T0331503

Big Data Analytics and Computing for Digital Forensic Investigations

Big Data Analytics and Computing for Digital Forensic Investigations

Edited by
Suneeta Satpathy
Biju Patnaik University of Technology, Bhubaneswar,
Odisha, India

Sachi Nandan Mohanty
ICFAI Foundation for Higher Education, Hyderabad,
Telangana, India

CRC Press
Taylor & Francis Group
Boca Raton London New York

CRC Press is an imprint of the
Taylor & Francis Group, an **informa** business

First edition published 2020
by CRC Press
6000 Broken Sound Parkway NW, Suite 300, Boca Raton, FL 33487-2742

and by CRC Press
2 Park Square, Milton Park, Abingdon, Oxon, OX14 4RN

ISBN: 978-0-367-45678-8 (hbk)
ISBN: 978-1-003-02474-3 (ebk)

Typeset in Minion Pro
by codeMantra

Visit the Taylor & Francis Web site at
http://www.taylorandfrancis.com

and the CRC Press Web site at
http://www.crcpress.com

Contents

Preface

DIGITAL FORENSICS AND ITS investigation have contemplated an archetype swing from a customary cellar access to an incorporated access in compilation, broadcasting and scrutiny of prearranged and shapeless information on the whole digital podium fortification and information safety. Nowadays, computer frauds and cybercrime have turn out to be a challenging task due to outsized quantity of data entry, inadequate crime examination modus operandi, rising dimension of data and cargo room capacity for digital examination. The theatrical exponential intensification of computer frauds and cybercrimes has gradually prolonged the research work in the field of digital forensics. Forensics has always been concerned with criminal cases, civil litigation and organization-initiated internal investigations. However, digital forensic investigation of computer frauds and cybercrimes differs from the normal crime investigation, in which the data in the form of 0's and 1's becomes digital evidence.

Digital evidence is of corroborative in nature in the virtual world of 0's and 1's. The fragile scenery of the digital evidence in the virtual world demonstrates its worth and examination from the digital investigation, thereby leading to the fact that finding the source of crime is well-thought-out domain of discourse in the digital forensic neighborhood. Due to storing data to drive organizational strategy, the exponential growth of big data systems over and over again identifies sales, health care sectors, academics domain and many different modes of electronic communication. Since digital investigation dispenses a huge quantity of hesitant information to diminish its qualms in the uncovering process, the forecaster has to assess a bulk of data brought together from diverse origins and unified databases. The forensic assessment of such statistics is palpable; if the records are worthy to an organization, then the information is precious to an investigation of that organization.

Digital forensics and its investigation involving big data require assortment and scrutiny of capacious heterogeneous data and its fine-tuning, filtration and broadcasting that can supplement the on-hand forensics corpse of knowledge and forensic investigative tools and techniques to handle the enormous, dispersed systems. Existing digital forensics investigational tools and well-defined models look for the evidence in mobile devices, stand-alone systems and laptops to gather and analyze unstructured data (e.g., email and document files). The digital investigation of any seized digital drive data demands the calculation of a MD5 or SHA-1 checksum. But with the challenges of big data, it is becoming insufficient to only let somebody to use traditional forensics tools. So the substitute methods for accumulating and examining such capacious data are the call for the hour.

Since digital forensics investigation is a data exhaustive examination and revelation, For improved investigation and uncovering, there is a need for these records to be synchronized and incorporated along with the fusion, correlation, aggregation and apparition practices for demonstrating a huge quantity of data straightaway by integrating valuable data from a variety of resources and assortment of crime uncovering criterion (e.g., menace types, invader actions and intention, consequences of the menace on resources). Integrated visualization of information distribution bars and rules, and revelation of behavior and broad analysis and charts allow investigating agencies to examine disparate regulations and facts at diverse echelon, among any breed of incongruity.

Big data is a paradigm shift in how data is stored and managed, and the same is true for digital forensic investigations of big data. There are many digital investigation models and approaches being developed to capture the digital evidence, but still its timely and accurate recovery, detection, aggregation, correlation and presentation are a distant dream. The field of digital forensics is large and continues to develop; in addition to their constant growth, big data machineries show the way to modify the apparatus and technologies employed for digital forensic explorations. Much work has been done to model digital investigation and to provide digital evidence, but a comprehensive correlated and aggregated merging of big data coming from different heterogeneous sources along with timely and accurate detection and analysis is the need of the hour. A fundamental understanding of digital forensics and its branches are important to examine the process and methods used in investigating digital information. Big data computing and digital forensics book will give the entire spectrum of digital forensics, its investigational tools, big data analytics and its involvement in digital forensics investigation.

Acknowledgments

T HE EDITORS WOULD LIKE to congratulate and thank all the authors for contributing their chapters, Dr. M.S. Rao, Mr. Sarat Chandra Satpathy, Dr. Sateesh Kumar Pradhan, Mr. Prasanta Parichha, Dr. Subhendu Kumar Pani, Dr. Bhagirathi Nayak, Mr. Ranjan Ganguli, Dr. Satyasundara Mahapatra, Mr. Chandrakant Mallick, Dr. Shweta Shankhwar, Ms. Anasuya Swain and Ms. Pallavi Mishra.

The editors would also like to extend a special thanks to Dr. Sarika Jain, Professor, Department of MCA, NIT, Kurukshetra, for her constant support of generating the turnitin report.

We would also like to thank the subject matter experts who could find their time to review the chapters and deliver those in time.

Finally, a ton of thanks to all the team members of CRC press for their dedicated support and help in publishing this edited book.

Editors

 **Dr. Suneeta Satpathy** received her PhD in computer science from Utkal University, Bhubaneswar, Odisha, in the year 2015, with Directorate of Forensic Sciences, MHA scholarship, from Government of India. She is currently working as an associate professor in the Department of Computer Science and Engineering at College of Engineering Bhubaneswar (CoEB), Bhubaneswar. Her research interests include computer forensics, cybersecurity, data fusion, data mining, big data analysis and decision mining. In addition to research, she has guided many postgraduate and graduate students. She has published papers in many international journals and conferences in repute. She has two Indian patents to her credit. Her professional activities include roles as editorial board member and/ or reviewer of *Journal of Engineering Science, Advancement of Computer Technology and Applications, Robotics and Autonomous Systems* (Elsevier) and *Computational and Structural Biotechnology Journal* (Elsevier). She is a life member of Computer Society of India (CSI), Indian Society For Technical Education (ISTE) and Odisha Information Technology Society (OITS).

 **Prof. Dr. Sachi Nandan Mohanty** received his postdoc in Cognitive Science from IIT Kanpur in the year 2019 and PhD in cognitive science from IIT Kharagpur in the year 2015, with MHRD scholarship from Government of India. He has recently joined as an associate professor in the Department of Computer Science and Engineering at ICFAI Foundation for Higher Education Hyderabad.

His research areas include data mining, big data analysis, cognitive science, fuzzy decision-making, brain–computer interface and computational intelligence. He has received three Best Paper Awards during his PhD at IIT Kharagpur from International Conference at Beijing, China, and the other at International Conference on Soft Computing Applications organized by IIT Roorkee in 2013. He has published 20 SCI journals. As a fellow of Indian Society Technical Education (ISTE), the Institute of Engineering and Technology (IET), and Computer Society of India (CSI), and member of Institute of Engineers and IEEE Computer Society, he is actively involved in the activities of the professional bodies/societies.

He has been bestowed with several awards, which include "Best Researcher Award" from Biju Patnaik University of Technology in 2019, "Best Thesis Award" (first Prize) from Computer Society of India in 2015, and "Outstanding Faculty in Engineering Award" from Department of Higher Education, Government of Odisha in 2020. He has received International Travel Fund from SERB, Department of Science and Technology, Government of India, to chair a session international conferences at the USA in 2020.

He is currently a reviewer of many journals such as *Journal of Robotics and Autonomous Systems* (Elsevier), *Computational and Structural Biotechnology* (Elsevier), *Artificial Intelligence Review* (Springer) and *Spatial Information Research* (Springer).

He has edited four books for CRC, Wiley and Springer Nature and also authored three books.

Contributors

Mr. Ranjan Ganguli is a double master degree holder and received his Master of Engineering in computer science and engineering from University Institute of Technology, Burdwan, West Bengal, in 2016. Presently, he is the founder and joint director of the company ISIKAN Consultancy Services Pvt. Ltd., Madhupur, Jharkhand. Formerly, he was the IT head in All India Institute of Local Self Government, Deoghar. He has more than ten years of teaching experience in undergraduate and postgraduate levels, including in Dr. Zakir Husain Institute, Deoghar. His research areas of interest include data mining, big data analytics, machine learning, software engineering, mathematics and other allied fields. He has recently published a paper in the journal *Research Directions Journal* (May 2019 issue). He is also the authorized information technology project coordinator of Sikkim Manipal University and guided several undergraduate- and postgraduate-level projects.

Prof. Raees Ahmad Khan has earned his PhD in software security from Jamia Millia Islamia, New Delhi, India. He is currently working as an associate professor and head of the Department of Information Technology, Babasaheb Bhimrao Ambedkar University (A Central University), Vidya Vihar, Raibareli Road, Lucknow, India. He has more than 25 years of teaching and research experience. His areas of interest include software security, software quality and software testing. He has published a number of national and international books, research papers, reviews and chapters on software security, software quality and software testing.

Dr. Satyasundara Mahapatra is an associate professor in the Department of Computer Science and Engineering, Pranveer Singh Institute of Technology, Kanpur, Uttar Pradesh. He received his master degree and PhD in computer science from Utkal University, Bhubaneswar, Odisha, in 2006 and 2016, respectively. He also holds a MCA degree from Utkal University, Bhubaneswar, Odisha, in 1997. His current research interests include machine learning, image processing, scheduling and IoT. He has authored or coauthored in international scientific journals, two book chapters and three patents' approval in his field of expertise.

Mr. Chandrakant Mallick is a PhD research scholar at Biju Patnaik University of Technology, Rourkela. He received his M.Tech degree in computer science in 2008 from Utkal University. He has several years of teaching and research experience. He is currently working as an assistant professor in the Department of Computer Science and Engineering, College of Engineering Bhubaneswar. He has contributed eight international research publications and a number of e-resources in cybersecurity for Odisha State Open University, Sambalpur. His current research interests include new-generation networks, with a special focus on social networks and applications, big data analytics and cybersecurity.

Ms. Pallavi Mishra received her M.Tech (IT) from Utkal University, Vani Vihar, Bhubaneswar, in 2019. She is perusing PhD at ICFAI Foundation, Hyderabad, India. Her first article titled as "Big Data Digital Forensics and Cyber Security" has been successfully approved for publication. Another article titled as "Development of Health Care System Using Soft Computing Techniques" is in the process of publication.

**Dr. Bhagirathi Nayak** is a competent, diligent, and result-oriented professional with an experience of 25 years at the IIT Kharagpur, India. He has been working in the field of computer science and engineering, bioinformatics and management, and been a database designer and developer; he is involved in teaching, academic administration and pedagogical activities. From August 2014, he is an associate professor, and head, in the Department of Information and Communication Technology, Sri Sri University, Cuttack. He did his both graduation and postgraduation in computer science with first class, and PhD also in computer science in the topic "Data Mining Algorithms for Fuzzy Association Rules in Large Database". Five PhD scholars who worked under his guidance are awarded, and another six PhD scholars are continuing under his guidance. His areas of interest include big data, data mining, big data analytics, artificial intelligence and machine learning.

He has received an award from Dr. A. P. J. Abdul Kalam Education and Research Centre, Government of India, for his contribution to data science on July 22, 2019, held at Hyderabad. He was also awarded Best Professor of Data Science in Odisha on August 18, 2019, at Bangalore, by India Education Award 2019. He did two international patents in the area of computer science and engineering.

He has visited several institutions, such as IIT Chennai, IIT Mumbai, IIT Delhi, ISI Bangalore, IIM Ahmadabad and IIM Kashipur. He has published more than 45 papers and international journals; most of them are published in Scopus and Thomson Reuter Indexing. He has written two books, which were published in Macmillan Publishers and Allied Publishers. He has also written two books on Linux operating systems and information security for Odisha State Open University.

He did many more consultancy projects from MHRD, Government of India; Bioinformatics, Department of Biotechnology, Government of India; Odisha Small Industry Corporation (OSIC), Cuttack; and Odisha Agro Industries Corporation Ltd. (OAIC), Bhubaneswar.

Recearchgate: www.researchgate.net/profile/Bhagirathi_Nayak

Linkedin: www.linkedin.com/in/drbnayak

Dr. Ananta Charan Ojha received his master degree in computer applications from Indira Gandhi Institute of Technology (IGIT), Sarang, Odisha, India, and a PhD in computer science from Utkal University, Bhubaneswar, India. He has around 25 years of experience in teaching computer science and information technology at undergraduate and postgraduate levels. He has been involved in teaching, research, curriculum development and academic administration.

He has guided several software development projects in MCA and B.Tech levels, and also guided around a dozen of M.Tech thesis. Presently, four PhD scholars are working under his guidance.

He has published more than 28 research articles/papers in referred conference proceedings and journals at national and international levels. He has been the consulting editor of *IUP Journal of Information Technology* published in ICFAI University Press since 2005.

His research interest lies in multi-agent systems, machine intelligence, data science, cyber physical systems and software engineering.

He has been associated with several conferences and provided professional services as a program committee member.

He is currently working as an associate professor in the Department of Computer Science & Engineering, Centurion University of Technology and Management, Bhubaneswar, Odisha, India. He can be reached at acojha@gmail.com.

Dr. Dhirendra Pandey is working as an assistant professor in the Department of Information Technology at Babasaheb Bhimrao Ambedkar University (BBAU). He has also served as an associate professor and head of the Department of Computer Science and Information Technology in the Satellite Campus of BBAU at Amethi. He has more than 15 years of teaching and research experience. He has published more than 65 research articles, 2 books, 8 book chapters and 3 patents. He received his PhD in computer science from Devi Ahilya Vishwavidyalaya in 2012 and M. Phil in computer science from Madurai Kamaraj University, Madurai, in 2008.

He has also executed a major research project from the Council of Science and Technology of Uttar Pradesh under Young Scientist Scheme. His research areas include software engineering, requirement engineering, software security and data mining.

Dr. Subhendu Kumar Pani received his PhD from Utkal University, Odisha, India, in 2013. He is working as a professor in the Department of Computer Science and Engineering and also a research coordinator at Orissa Engineering College (OEC), Bhubaneswar. He has more than 16 years of teaching and research experience. His research areas of interest include data mining, big data analysis, web data analytics, fuzzy decision-making and computational intelligence. He is the recipient of five researcher awards. In addition to research, he has guided 1 PhD student and 31 M.Tech students. He has published 51 international journal papers (19 Scopus indexes). His professional activities include roles as associate editor, editorial board member and/or reviewer of various international journals. He is associated with a number of conference societies. He has published more than 100 international journals, 5 authored books, 2 edited books and 10 book chapters to his credit. He is a fellow of SSARSC and a life member of IE, ISTE, ISCA, OBA, OMS, SMIACSIT, SMUACEE and CSI.

Mr. Prasanta Kumar Parichha (MA, PGDCFS, PGDCS, PGDHR, CLP, CCPP) has been working as a constable in Odisha Police for the past 17 years. He has completed master degrees in public administration and criminology, and postgraduate diplomas in cyber security, human rights and forensic science. He has also completed various massive open online courses (MOOCs) on digital forensics and related disciplines. He received a "Cyber Crime Investigation Training Excellence Award" from National Cyber Security Bureau (NCSB), Hyderabad, in 2018. He is also a part-time academic counselor for a diploma program in cybersecurity at Odisha State Open University. He is a police officer by profession and a cybersecurity researcher by passion.

Dr. Sateesh Kumar Pradhan is currently working as a professor at Postgraduate Department of Computer Science at Utkal University, Bhubaneswar. He completed his master's degree in 1983 and PhD in 1999. He has published his research work in the areas of neural computing, computer architecture, mobile computing and data mining in several journals and conferences. He has also written many books in his areas of interest and edited many textbooks for Government of Odisha. He has been honored with various accolades from time to time for his contribution to the field of computer science. He is also heading various honorary positions at Utkal University as well as other universities of Odisha.

Dr. M. S. Rao was the ex-director and chief forensic scientist of Directorate of Forensic Science Services – Government of India for about eight years and retired in the year 2009. He has been a professor and scientific advisor to Gujarat Forensic Science University. He began his professional career at State Forensic Science Laboratory, Bhubaneswar, in 1975. He became the director of Central Forensic Science Laboratory – Kolkata in 1993 and continued at the post for around eight years. During his eight years of service as the chief forensic scientist of the India, he held several highly commendable jobs, including upgradation of Forensic Science Services at both Central and State levels; introduced forensic science education at a number of universities and colleges, across the country, providing logistics support to sustain the course; launching forensic awareness programs for police, judiciary, prosecutors and medico-legal experts at almost all state and central forensic science laboratories; strengthening new high-tech forensic disciplines such as DNA profiling, computer forensics, audio forensics and video forensics, brain wave analysis, firearms digital signature identification system, and tele-forensics; and introducing and implementing the concept of sending forensic experts to major crime scenes.

Mr. Sarat Chandra Satpathy completed his M.Sc. in zoological science in 1973 at Utkal University, Odisha. Then, he joined as a scientific officer in Forensic Science Laboratory, Odisha, in 1975. During his professional career, he has worked in various scientific examinations of crime cases in state as well as in regional laboratories. He has contributed greatly to the criminal justice delivery system in forensic science history of the state. After a successful service career, he retired as a joint director, State Forensic Science Laboratory, in 2008.

Dr. Shweta Shankhwar completed her doctorate in the field of cybersecurity in 2019 from Babasaheb Bhimrao Ambedkar University (A Central University), Lucknow. She has been a gold medalist and well accomplished in all her academic performances during her postgraduation from Babasaheb Bhimrao Ambedkar University (A Central University), Lucknow. Her areas of interest include cyber frauds, cybersecurity, phishing and machine learning. Her notable works include 22 widely cited research papers published by different well-known and reputed publishers and magazines. She is currently involved in teaching and research, and also takes a deep interest in sharing her knowledge with common people, teachers, industry and police from different platforms such as seminars and workshops in colleges and university campuses.

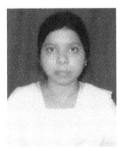

Ms. Anasuya Swain (MBA, MPhil., UGC NET and JRF) is working as an assistant professor at the College of Engineering Bhubaneswar. She has more than 60 International and National Publications and one book to her credit.

CHAPTER 1

Introduction to Digital Forensics

Prasanta Kumar Parichha

Odisha Police

CONTENTS

1.1 DIGITAL FORENSICS OVERVIEW

Crime is as old as humankind. Most crimes leave traces of evidence. Although the Internet has revolutionized digital technology by encouraging business opportunities at an alarming rate, insecurity exposes serious threats and vulnerabilities [1]. As the Internet has evolved, so have the avenues where users have another part of their digital life ranging from payments to social networking and from e-commerce to dating. We may say all our data are now in cyberspace and most vulnerable to hackers' target. With the development of computer systems, the world has also witnessed the emergence of cybercrime.

Digital forensics is a process used to tackle the challenges of analyzing and handling big data during unlawful time, and preserving the forensic principles to be presented in the court of law as digital evidence, transmitted from or stored on computers. Big data is a challenge for digital forensics to ensure safety measures [2,3]. Digital forensics faces major challenges, identifying necessary proof as of a big dataset. The huge dataset obtained as a consequence of the application of digital forensics on big data requires proper management.

Digital forensics is a discipline that involves investigation and analysis techniques to gather and preserve evidence from a particular electronic or digital device and to present as such in the court of law for prosecution. The goal of cyber forensics is to perform a structured investigation while maintaining the integrity of evidence and a documented chain of custody [1]. Thus, it plays a vital role in cybercrime investigation. Ultimately, the fields of information security, which focuses on protecting information and assets, and computer forensics, which focuses on the response to hi-tech offenses, started to intertwine [4]. Acquiring disk images is the first step in preserving digital forensic evidence in preparation for postmortem examination and analysis. Most criminal investigations span country borders and involve multiple jurisdictions [1,4,5].

1.1.1 Definitions of Digital Forensics

In *Forensic Magazine*, Ken Zatyko defined digital forensics as "the application of computer science and investigation procedures for a legal purpose involving the analysis of digital evidence after proper search authority, chain of custody, validation with mathematics, use of validated tools, repeatability, reporting, and possible expert presentation" [2,6,7].

1.1.2 The 3A's of Digital Forensics Methodology

The 3A's of digital forensics methodologies are as follows: (i) Acquire evidence without modification or corruption, (ii) authenticate that the recovered evidence is the same as the originally seized data and (iii) analyze data without any alterations. Digital forensics includes the analysis of images, videos and audio (in both analog and digital formats). The focus of this kind of analysis is generally authenticity, comparison and enhancement.

1.1.3 The History of Digital Forensics

The history of digital forensics is short compared to that of other scientific disciplines [1,2,6].

- The growth of home computers in 1980 and dial-up Bulletin Board System services triggered in computer forensics within law enforcement agencies. The Federal Bureau of Investigation (FBI) developed a pioneering program to analyze the types of computer evidence in 1984.

- AccessData was developed in 1987. The increased abuse and Internet-based attacks led to the formation of Computer Emergency Response Team (CERT).

- The FBI hosted the first International Conference on Computer Evidence (IOCE), held at Quantico in 1993 and was attended by representatives of 26 nations.

- In 1998, IOCE was commissioned by the G8 to establish international guidelines, protocols and procedures for digital evidence.

- In 2002, The Scientific Working Group on Digital Evidence (SWGDE) published their work "Best Practices for Computer Forensics".

- During the Budapest Convention on Cybercrime, relevant topics such as copyright infringement, child pornography and fraud were discussed.

- The ISO published ISO 17025 guidelines for the competence of testing and calibrating laboratories in 2005.

- Gradually, the Cyber Forensic Tools started to make their stride: EnCase by Guidance Software and Forensic Toolkit (FTK) by Access Data. Then, some Open Source Intelligence Tools such as Sleuth Kit and Autopsy for Linux came in the picture. Not only did the ever-increasing rate of cybercrimes, from phishing to hacking and stealing of personal information, confine to a particular country but also globally at large, there is a need for forensic experts to be available in public and private organizations [8].

We all will agree to the fact that we are depending more and more on Information and Communication Technology (ICT) tools and Internet for digital services to an extent that today we talk online using chat applications, we depend on email to communicate with relatives and in offices, we stay in touch with our friends and update status using social engineering platforms like Facebook, we work online by staying connected to our office/client using Internet, we shop online, we teach online, we learn online and we submit our bill online today. Our dependency on computer and Internet has increased so much that we are "online" most of the time. Therefore, there is an increased need of protecting our information from being misused by following the information security guidelines. However, if the security of our computer is compromised, computer forensics comes in handy for post-incident investigation.

1.1.4 The Objectives of Digital Forensics

The objectives of digital forensics are to provide guidelines for

- Following the first responder procedure and accessing the victim's computer after the incident.

- Designing full-proof procedures at a suspected crime scene to ensure the authenticity of digital evidence.

- Performing data acquisition and duplication.

- Recovering deleted files and deleted partitions from digital media to extract the evidence and validate them.

- Analyzing digital media to preserve evidence, analyzing logs and deriving conclusions, investigating network traffics and logs to correlate events, investigating wireless and web attacks, tracking emails and investigating email crimes.

- Producing a computer forensic report that provides a complete report investigation process.

- Preserving the evidence and maintaining the chain of custody.

- Employing the hard and correct procedures necessary to stand up in a court of law.

- Presenting opinion in the court of law as an expert witness.

1.2 DIGITAL EVIDENCE

Digital evidence is defined as information and data of value to an investigation that is stored on, received or transmitted by an electronic device. Digital evidence, by its very nature, is fragile and can be altered, damaged or destroyed by improper handling or examination. Forensic examination is best conducted on a copy of the original evidence. The original evidence should be acquired in a manner that protects and preserves the integrity of the evidence [1,4,9].

The term "digital evidence" is explained by Casey (2004) as "Digital evidence or electronic evidence is any probative information stored or transmitted in digital form that a party to a court case may use at trial". However, before accepting the pieces of evidence, the court may verify whether the same is relevant evidence or authentic or hearsay evidence. As such, digital evidence may also include electronic records.

The term "electronic record" has been explained by the Information Technology Act, 2000 (amended in 2008), as follows: Electronic record means data recorded or data generated, image or sound stored, received or sent in an electronic form, or microfilm or computer-generated microfiche. Section 3 of the Indian Evidence Act explains the definition of evidence in all documents, including electronic records produced for the inspection of the court. Section 4 of the Information Technology Act states the following: "Where any law provides that information or any other matter shall be in writing or in the typewritten or printed form, then, notwithstanding

DIGITAL EVIDENCES

FIGURE 1.1   Sources of digital evidence.

anything contained in such law, such requirement shall be deemed to have been satisfied if such information or matter is (a) rendered or made available in an electronic form and (b) accessible so as to be usable for a subsequent reference".

The digital devices typically store vast amounts of data (Figure 1.1). Some of these are active, and others may be residual or backup data. Digital pieces of evidence are of two types: (i) **Volatile evidence** includes memory, networks, running process and open files, and (ii) **non-volatile evidence** includes hard drives, CD/DVD and USB.

1.2.1 Active Data

- Active data contains current files on the computer, those still in directories and available to all applications.

- Active data consists of user-created data such as customer information, inventory data, word-processing documents or spreadsheets, programs and operating system files, including temporary files, recycle bin files, Internet history directory, "cookie jar" and system registry files.

- Active data would be similar to interviewing all the witnesses present at a crime scene when the investigation officer arrives.

- Active data can be password-protected or encrypted requiring further forensic analysis.

- At the crime scene, the forensic expert can find clues that are left in plain sight and are easily retrievable.

1.2.2 Archival Data

- This is data that's been transferred or backed up to peripheral media such as tapes, CDs, ZIP disks, floppy disks, network services or the Internet.

- In the crime scene scenario, archival data would be the surveillance video removed from the security camera installed and taken during the occurrence of crime.

- Detectives would need to examine the active and latent data available at the scene to determine what archival data had left the scene.

- In computer forensics, we can identify archival data by examining the target hard drive to determine files that have been copied off the hard disk.

1.2.3 Latent Data

- Latent data is also called ambient data consisting of deleted files and other data, including memory "dumps" that have "lodged in the digital cracks", but can still be retrieved. Latent data also includes the following:

  Swap files: A file on a hard disk used to provide space for programs that have been transferred from the processor's memory.

  Temporary files: Files created to contain temporary information while a new file is being made.

  Printer spool files: An image file created every time a document is printed.

  Metadata: It provides information about who, what, where, when and how regarding a file's creation, modification or deletion.

- Finding latent data at a crime scene would not be possible without the use of a crime scene technician. Similarly, specialized computer forensic examiners use software tools to obtain information from a suspect's hard drive.

1.2.4 Residual Data

Residual data refers to data that is not active on a computer system. It includes data found on media free space and file slack space, and data within files that has functionally been deleted in that it is not visible using the application with which the file was created, without the use of undelete or special data recovery techniques.

Most users think that deleting files from a computer actually removes all the files, but in fact a computer's OS keeps a directory of the name and location of each file. When a user deletes a file, the OS doesn't remove the file data. Rather, it only indicates that the space is available. The contents of a deleted file remain in place until specialized programs overwrite them. A person, who knows how to access these released but not erased areas and who has the proper tools, can recover their contents. Residual data can also include portions of files distributed on the drive surface or embedded within other files. These files are commonly referred to as file fragments or unallocated data.

1.3 BRANCHES OF DIGITAL FORENSICS

Digital forensics has several sub-branches related to the investigation of various types of cybercrimes, as shown in Figure 1.2. These branches include the following [1,2,6]:

1.3.1 Computer Forensics

Computer forensics refers to using forensic techniques for retrieving evidence from computers. The goal of computer forensics is to explain the current state of a digital artifact, such as a computer system, storage medium or electronic document.

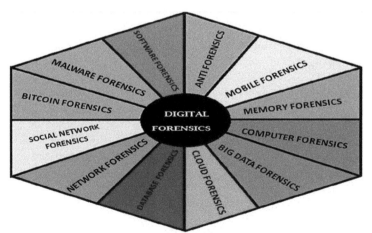

BRANCHES OF DIGITAL FORENSICS

FIGURE 1.2   Digital forensic branches.

According to Juniper Research, cybercrime losses to businesses will surpass $2 trillion. With data breaches occurring all around the world every day, the demand for digital forensic experts is increasing.

The term "forensics" literally means using some sort of established scientific process for the collection, analysis and presentation of the evidence which has been collected. However, all forms of evidence are important, especially when a cyberattack has occurred. Thus, a formal definition of computer forensics can be presented as follows:

"It is the discipline that combines the elements of law and computer science to collect and analyze data from computer systems, networks, wireless communications, and storage devices in a way that is admissible as evidence in a court of law". Computer forensics to a business or a corporation is of paramount importance.

1.3.2 Network Forensics

Network forensics is a sub-branch of digital forensics that revolves around examining networking-related digital evidence. It involves monitoring, recording, analyzing and interpreting network traffic for the purposes of information gathering, evidence collection or intrusion detection. The major components of network forensics include packet capture and analysis, network device acquisition and incident response. Network forensics has become a crucial component of the IT industry as they are very concerned about their data protection from cyberattacks [6].

The network forensic artifacts provide evidence or insight into network communication. It can be generated from the DHCP servers, DNS servers, Web Proxy servers, IDS, IPS and firewalls. It also includes evidence from software-based firewalls and mail clients such as MS Outlook, Outlook Express and Eudora. Apart from commercial tools, there is a rich treasury of open source tools such as Wireshark, Xplico and Network Miner.

1.3.3 Software Forensics

Software forensics is aimed at authorship analysis of computer source code for legal purposes. It involves the areas of author identification, discrimination and characterization. These remnants may take many forms, including programming language source files, shell scripts, executable codes, object files, changes made to existing programs or even a text file drafted by the hackers.

1.3.4 Mobile Forensics

As per research, most of the cybercrimes are committed through mobiles. Mobile forensics is the recovery of digital evidence from mobile devices. It can be related to any digital device, which has both internal memory and communication ability. It includes Personal Digital Assistant, GPS and tablets. Through mobile devices, we can access various personal information such as contacts, photos, calendars and notes, SMS and MMS messages. Smartphones additionally contain video, email, web browsing information, location information, and social networking chat messages and contacts [4,5,7].

There is a growing need for mobile forensics due to several reasons, and some of the prominent reasons are as follows:

- Use of mobile phones to store and transmit personal and corporate information.

- Use of mobile phones in online transactions.

- Law enforcement, criminals and mobile phone devices.

Types of evidence found on mobile devices are not only limited to memory, SIM or SD card, but also include the information gathered from smartphone such as cloud storage, browser history and geo locations. Evidential and technical challenges exist. A detailed list of evidence on mobile devices will include the following:

- Subscriber and equipment identifiers.

- Date/time, language and other settings.

- Phone book/contact information.

- Calendar information.

- Text messages.

- Outgoing, incoming and missed call logs.

- Electronic mail.

- Photos.

- Audio and video recordings.

- Multimedia messages.

- Instant messaging.

- Web browsing activities.

- Electronic documents.

- Social media-related data.

- Application-related data.

- Location information.

- Geolocation data.

1.3.5 Memory Forensics

Memory forensics is to identify unauthorized and anomalous suspicious activity on a target computer or server. This is usually achieved by running special software that captures the current state of the system's memory as a snapshot file, also known as a memory dump. This file can be taken off-site and searched by the forensic expert. The best memory forensic tools are Belkasoft RAM Capture, Process Hacker, Volatility Suite, Rekall and Helix ISO.

Some of the memory acquisition types include the following:

- *Pagefile*: This is a file that stores similar information that is stored in your system RAM.

- *VMware snapshot*: This is a snapshot of a virtual machine, which saves its state as it was at the exact moment that the snapshot was granted.

- *RAW format*: It is extracted from a live cyber environment.

- *Crash dump*: Information is gathered by the operating system running in the system.

- *Hibernation file*: It is a saved snapshot that the operating system can return to after hibernating.

1.3.6 Malware Forensics

There are different types of malware (malicious software) that infect users and steal their personal information such as name, address, location, email id, phone number and other special identities like social media login passwords. The hackers inject malwares such as adware, spyware, virus, worm,

Trojan, rootkit, backdoor, key logger, browser hijacker and ransomware to access the detailed credentials.

Malware analysis is of two types:

- *Static malware analysis*: It entails the investigation of executable files without going through the actual instructions.

- *Dynamic malware analysis*: It executes malware to observe its activities, comprehend its functionality and identify technical indicators that can be used in revealing signatures.

1.3.7 Database Forensics

Database forensics relates to the reconstruction of metadata and page information from within a dataset. It normally uses a read-only method or an identical forensic copy of the data when interfacing with a database to ensure that no data is compromised. Oracle, MySQL, Microsoft SQL server, PostgresSQL and MongoDB are some of the popular databases. Database servers store sensitive information such as schema, database log, file system (metadata), trigger, storage engine and data structure (Figure 1.3).

1.3.8 Social Network Forensics

Most of the present-day crimes are social media related. Social networking forensics is the application of virtual investigation and analysis techniques. Online social media such as Facebook and Twitter monitor and store information, and analyze and preserve the types of digital evidence.

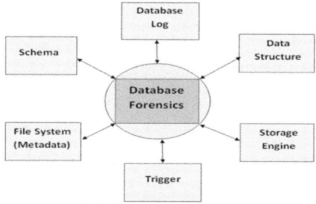

source : https://ars.els-cdn.com/content/image/1-s2.0-S1742287619300143-gr2.jpg

FIGURE 1.3 Database server.

1.3.9 Anti-Forensics

Anti-forensics is an attempt to manipulate data and erase data. So, it is quite a difficult task for the forensic experts to examine the resulting delay in investigation. Some of the anti-forensics techniques are encryption of data using steganography, modification of metadata, manipulation of timestamps, tunneling, Tor browsing, wiping a drive, etc.

1.3.10 Cloud Forensics

Cloud computing includes network service that interacts with over the network. The private cloud, public cloud, community cloud, hybrid cloud and distributed cloud are the deployment models of cloud computing. Iaas (infrastructure as a service), PaaS (platform as a service) and SaaS (software as a service) are the three service models of cloud computing.

1.3.11 Bit Coin Forensics

Bit coin is one type of crypto currency, which is used for easy and anonymous transactions. It is a decentralized block chain based. Dark net sites include Dream, Outlaw, Silk Road, Real Deal, Black Market Reloaded, Black Bank, Pandora, Sheep, Tor Bazaar and Pirate Market. Block chain and other alternative coins can be tracked using one of the several block chain explorers. The bit coin forensics is a challenging issue.

1.3.12 Big Data Forensics

Big data is the pool of potential knowledge organizations use for ongoing discovery and analysis. The information contained in big data comes in different forms: unstructured data and multi-structured data [3,10].

Big data is generated through three main sources:

- *Transactional* information resulting from payments, invoices, storage records and delivery notices.

- *Machine data* gathered through the equipment itself like web logs or smartphone sensors.

- *Social data* found in social media activity, such as tweets or Facebook likes.

1.4 PHASES OF FORENSIC INVESTIGATION PROCESS

The following five topics describe the necessary basic phases to conduct a digital forensic examination (Figure 1.4) and suggest the order in which they should be conducted [7,8]. Although document presentation is listed

FIGURE 1.4 Phases of digital forensic examination.

as the last step, a well-trained examiner understands that documentation is continuous throughout the entire examination process.

1.4.1 Readiness

The following ten steps describe the key activities in implementing a forensic readiness program.

1. Define the crime scenario that requires digital evidence.

2. Identify available sources and different types of potential evidence.

3. Determine the evidence collection requirement.

4. Establish a capacity for securely gathering legally admissible evidence to meet the requirement.

5. Establish a policy for secure storage and handling of potential evidence.

6. Ensure monitoring is targeted to detect and deter major incidents.

7. Specify circumstances when escalation to a full formal investigation (which may use the digital evidence) should be launched.

8. Train staff in incident awareness, so that all those involved understand their role in the digital evidence process and the legal sensitivities of evidence.

9. Document an evidence-based case describing the incident and its impact.

10. Ensure legal review to facilitate action in response to the incident.

Prof. A. Pooe and L. Labuschgne [8] developed a conceptual model for digital forensics readiness (Figure 1.5).

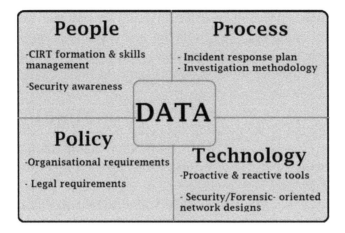

FIGURE 1.5   Conceptual model for digital forensic readiness.

a. *People*: Under the people category are many sub-activities such as the hiring of the experienced cyber incident response team members, segregation of duties, security training and awareness campaigns. The objective is to ensure the human resource management toward the prevention and detection of crime.

b. *Process*: The process category is concerned with activities that ensure the integrity of evidence. This includes ensuring that operational documents such as incident response plan and a forensic methodology are in place.

c. *Policy*: The six categories of policies that facilitate digital forensics are retaining information, planning the response, training, accelerating the investigation, preventing anonymous activities and protecting the evidence.

d. *Technology*: An organization needs to ensure that appropriate technology is used not only to enable business operations, but also to prevent and detect computer incidents.

1.4.2 Identification

The Locard's exchange principle postulates that when two objects come in contact, they leave a trace on each other. In the digital crime scene, we often have trace evidence when two systems come into contact with each other [1,7,8]. For example, if an individual browses a website, the web server or web application firewall may record the individual's IP address within a collection log. The website may also deposit a cookie on the laptop. Just as in the physical world, evidence exchanged in this manner may be temporary and our ability to observe it may be limited to the tools and knowledge we currently have.

Identification is a crucial step in the forensic examination process. It directly affects efforts to develop a plan of action and ultimately the success of the investigation. Before starting any forensic examination, the scope of actions must be identified, including the prime suspects, best sources of evidence and costs required. It should be noted that the threat actors very easily manipulate digital evidence, so reliance on a single piece of digital evidence without other corroborating evidence should always be tempered with caution and should be verified before it can be trusted.

1.4.3 Collection

Digital evidence, by its very nature, is fragile and can be altered, damaged or destroyed by improper handling or examination. For these reasons, special precautions should be taken to preserve this type of evidence. Failure to do so may render it unusable or lead to an inaccurate conclusion. The collection element is where the digital forensic examiners begin the process of acquiring the digital evidence [1,2,10,11]. *The Internet Engineering Task Force (IETF)* has put together a document titled *Guidelines for Collection and Archiving (RFC 3227)* that addresses the order of volatility of digital evidence:

- Registers, cache.

- Routing table, ARP cache, process table, kernel statistics and memory (RAM).

- Temporary file systems.

- Disk.

- Remote logging and monitoring data.

- Physical configuration, network topology.

- Archival media.

It is imperative that digital forensic examiners take this volatility into account when starting the process of evidence collection. Methods should be employed where volatile evidence will be collected and moved on to a non-volatile medium such as an external hard drive.

Intentional or accidental modification of data during the acquisition and preservation stage should be avoided, and in case it occurs, record the changes made in the system. Make the storage devices write-protect in order to accidentally overwrite the data. After bringing the digital media to the forensics laboratory, a proper chain of custody should be maintained and these types of evidence should be stored in a physically safe location with access control facility. Also, enough duplicate copies of the media should be made to carry out the investigation.

1.4.4 Analysis

Extraction refers to the recovery of data from the media. Analysis refers to the interpretation of the recovered data and placement of it in a logical and useful format. After the process of collection, the evidence is taken for forensic analysis by a forensic examiner to look out for findings that can support or oppose the matters in the investigation. During the analysis, the forensic examiner should maintain the integrity of the digital evidence.

1.4.5 Presentation

A forensic examiner will be required to prepare a detailed written report, which addresses every action and captures the critical data required. This report should be thorough, accurate, and without opinion or bias. This report will be made part of a larger incident investigation and aids in determining the root cause of the crime [3].

Another aspect of the presentation is the role that the forensic examiner might play in a criminal or civil proceeding. Testifying in court may be required if the incident under investigation has yielded a suspect or other responsible party. It is during this testimony that the forensic examiner will be required to present the facts of the forensic examination in much the same dispassionate manner as the report. The examiner will be required to present the facts and conclusions without bias and may be limited as to what opinions they testify to. Some may be limited to presenting the facts of the examination. Other times, as examiners acquire skills and have been deemed an expert witness, they may be able to offer an opinion.

All these documents may be presented for trial in the court of law.

- Take notes when consulting with the case investigator and/or prosecutor.

- Maintain a copy of the search authority with the case notes.

- Maintain the initial request for assistance with the case file.

- Maintain a copy of chain of custody documentation.

- Take all notes in detail.

- Documentation of date, time stamp and complete description, including action taken report.

- Documentation of irregularities noticed during investigation.

- Documentation of network topology, all user login id and passwords.

- Documentation of network modifications.

- Documentation of OS, running apps, etc.

- Crime scene documentation about storage, remote logins and backups.

1.4.5.1 Chain of Custody

The chain of custody refers to the forensic link and the proper bit-by-bit documentation of electronic evidence to produce it authentically in the court of law. The sample format is shown in Figure 1.6.

Some procedures of maintaining chain of custody include the following:

- Save the original material.

- Take photos of physical evidence.

- Take screenshots of digital evidence content.

- Document date, time and other information of receipt.

Description of Evidence		
Item #	Quantity	Description of Item (Model, Serial #, Condition, Marks, Scratches)
Chain of Custody				
Item #	Date/Time	Released by (Signature & ID#)	Received by (Signature & ID#)	Comments/Location

FIGURE 1.6 Chain of custody format.

1.5 CONCLUSION

The large-scale implementation of big data analytics is yet to take place. Our lives are entangled in the matrix of big data being created in cyberspace. The need for digital forensics has grown to a larger extent due to the presence of a majority of digital documents. The investigators must practice to minimize the option of examining the original evidence. They must be fully aware of all the steps involved in the investigative process.

REFERENCES

1. NIJ Special Report (2004), Forensic Examination of Digital Evidence: A Guide for Law Enforcement.
2. J. Sammons (2012), *The Basics of Digital Forensics*, ISBN-978-1-59749-661-2.
3. P. Thenmozhi, N. Maraimalai (2016), Big Data and Cyber Crimes: Prevention and Risks.
4. Accessed from www.coursehero.com.
5. Accessed from Ipubuzz.files.wordpress.com.
6. N. Reddy (2019), *Practical Cyber Forensics*, Springer Science and Business Media LLC, Berlin, Germany.
7. R. Rowlingson (2004), A ten step process for forensic readiness. *International Journal of Digital Evidence*, 2, 12–18.
8. A. Pooe, L. Labuschgne (2012), A Conceptual Model for Digital Forensics Readiness. www.researchgate.net/publication/261265748.
9. Accessed from resources.infosecinstitute.com.
10. P. K. Parichha (2019), Cyber crime investigation: A big challenge before the law enforcement in India. *Digital 4n6 Journal*, 6, 12–19.
11. ePGPathasala Portal, MHRD, Government of India. (2017), Cyber Criminology and Cyber Forensics Module.

CHAPTER 2

Digital Forensics and Digital Investigation to Form a Suspension Bridge Flanked by Law Enforcement, Prosecution, and Examination of Computer Frauds and Cybercrime

M.S. Rao
Gujarat Forensic Science University

Sarat Chandra Satpathy
Odisha State Forensic Science Lab

CONTENTS

2.1 FORENSIC SCIENCE AND DIGITAL FORENSICS

Forensic science is a branch of science that makes use of technology for investigating the related facts so that the respective crime is proved and criminal is punished. Forensics does the examination and discovery of hidden evidence by applying scientific methods keeping the rules and regulations of LAW intact [1–3]. It can be better described as "Application of SCIENCE to COURT OF LAW" mainly based on Locard's principle, which states "Whenever you do something you leave something (evidence) at crime site and get something (evidence) with you" [1,2,4].

2.2 DIGITAL FORENSICS

Digital forensics is the obscure part of digital fraud investigation process [4]. Digital forensics follows the philosophy of traditional forensic discipline to establish and recover corroborative digital evidence. Digital forensics refers to the extraction of potential digital evidence from the data contained in digital electronic media devices for the precise attainment scrutiny and perpetuation of data presentation in the court of law with the use of computer science methods, tools and techniques. Digital forensics is classified into different areas, such as computer forensics, network forensics and software forensics. Digital forensics discipline can be further segmented into a variety of disciplines such as video, audio, image, disk and memory forensics [2,3,5]. Computer forensics searches for the digital evidence where standalone computers have been used to commit computer frauds and cybercrime [5], and network forensics deals with identifying and preventing threats into network-interconnected systems and scrutinizing potential legal digital evidence after a digital threat has occurred [1]. Software forensics allows us to become aware of the instigator of the malevolent code.

2.2.1 Digital Evidence

In this era of digital technology, more shares of digital threat evidence are inherent in the digital devices though major shares of such corroboration are still in use for the consignment of conventional crimes. Digital evidence exists in the form of 0's and 1's and is fragile and unique in comparison with paper-based evidence [6,7]. Digital evidence may be present in locations, which are hidden, unknown, unusual and unfamiliar to its users. Such property of digital evidence allows it to be easily contaminated or cleaned out and can be reproduced [7].

Accordingly, the output of digital forensic investigation is the fragile digital evidence, which requires proper preservation; on the other hand, analyzing the digital media needs the creation of carbon copy to guarantee the authenticity and acceptability in the court of law. As the Digital Age is progressing exponentially and integrating itself in day-to-day life stuffs, new interrogation and provocations are persistently budding [1,6,7]. The output of digital forensic investigation has to gratify the following attributes in order to be permissible in the court of law.

- **Acceptable**: The digital evidence has to follow certain legal rules in order to be presented before the court of law.

- **Bona fide**: It should have the potential to strap the digital evidentiary data to the digital crime confrontation by establishing the relativity.

- **Absolute**: It should be able to trace back digital crime story in both the angles – to prove the cybercriminal's actions and to demonstrate his or her innocence.

- **Consistent**: The digital evidence should not carry any confusion or doubt to prove its legitimacy and sincerity.

- **Plausible and explicable**: The potential legal digital evidence should be voluntarily credible and comprehensible by a court of law.

Digital evidence can stay in the form of active evidence and residual evidence as shown in Figure 2.1.

The active digital evidence is directly noticeable to the operating system and its users. The active evidence examples may include all types of files that are created by the computer users, such as document files and spreadsheet files. It can be directly accessible from the seized hard drives. However, the residual digital evidence is the digital data that is indirectly

FIGURE 2.1   Types of digital evidence.

present in the storage media drives because it has been either deleted or hidden by the cybercriminals. It can be recovered by the investigative toolkits as the users are unaware of the fact that the system only deletes the pointer pointing to the respective file location, not the entire content of the file. The fragments of the respective file can be obtained from the slack space or swap space of the storage media drives.

2.3 SEGMENTS OF DIGITAL FORENSICS

Digital forensic science is different from the traditional forensic disciplines [2,8]; that is, it requires the examination to be performed virtually in a restricted environment; as a result, the investigation ends with the information that may prove the trepidation or certainty of cybercriminals.

Digital forensic investigations can be segmented into four phases: preparation, compilation, assessment and post-assessment [1–3,7,8].

2.3.1 Preparation

This phase is more toward spreading awareness what is to be done if a digital crime occurs.

2.3.1.1 An Investigative Plan

Digital forensic investigators have to write the strategy plans for carrying out the investigation in an investigation testimony. This testimony sketches out identification and assessment of resources, development of investigative procedures, assignment of roles and responsibilities, and selection of risk assessment strategies and equipment to carry out the investigation in the crime scene.

2.3.1.2 Training and Testing

Digital forensic investigators are trained about the process of carrying out the identification, searching, collection, handling and transportation of electronic evidence. The important attributes of digital forensics are the sincerity and integrity of digital evidence having an investigative value that uses electronic devices such as audio, video, cell phones and digital fax machines for their transmission. Since the digital evidence is fragile in nature, the digital forensic investigators have to be properly trained to handle it.

2.3.1.3 Equipment

The inspectional equipment, such as video cameras, digital cameras, software toolkits and other tools, must be well versed among the digital forensic investigators for the smooth advancement of investigational stepladders.

2.4 COMPILATION

The collection phase comes into play when the digital crime incident is detected through various security-tracking systems such as intrusive behavior identification, tracking of audit trails, complaints, profile detection, abnormal behavior detection, monitoring of log activities and any other means.

2.4.1 Evidence Search and Collection

Digital forensic data custody requires creating an exact replica of the questioned system disk drive and examination of all active and residual data from memory, registers as well as network behavioral states. The registers, cache memory and memory and transitory files, operational processes and dynamic networking tables are required to be investigated to collect the evidential data.

2.4.2 Data Recovery

Data recovery plays an important role in digital forensic investigation. Data can be recovered from all the hardware and software components of the system by creating the exact replica of digital media drives in the first step. Replication of the digital media involves the construction of a bit-for-bit copy of custody digital media to provide an ineffaceable true copy on which various analytical experiments can be performed, without touching the original digital media drives.

2.4.3 Assessment

Assessing the data is the third vital segment in the digital forensic investigation because in this phase, digital forensic inspectors settle on all WH questions such as whether the digital crime act has happened, when and how it has happened and the consequential brunt with the executor. This phase would find a pathway to the exact truth along with the potential legal digital evidence by analyzing each minute level of raw data. Suspected data are examined and analyzed using the techniques of fusion, correlation, graphing, mapping or time lining to establish and discover associations within the data for forming an exploratory hypothesis.

2.4.4 Post-Assessment

The collection of potential digital evidence involving extraction, interpretation and confirmation followed by the presentation is handed over to the court of law for further action, and the seized data is returned to its owner. The court of law aspires the digital evidence to have uprightness, genuineness and reproductiveness along with non-interference and minimization attributes.

2.5 STEPLADDER OF DIGITAL FORENSIC INVESTIGATION MODEL

Digital investigation uses science and technology to carry out the inspections of the past events with an aim to find potential digital evidence that can trace the digital crime back to its source or origin telling the whole story how it happened and who has done it. The rationale behind the digital inspection is to unearth digital data associated with the incidents under exploration and represent those to the fact finder. The investigation follows a defined approach in the form of digital investigation models. Many models have been developed based on three constituents that Kruse and Heiser [9] refer to crime investigations. The basic components of investigational modeling can be summarized as getting hold of the evidence with integrity preservation, substantiating the legitimacy of the evidentiary extraction and exploring the data to locate the points of interest with its integrity being maintained.

The digital forensic investigation [4,10] includes the achievable sources of evidence (such as eyewitness proclamation, credentials, corporal evidence like any biological prints) and data present in seized digital disk drives. Once the digital forensic investigation is accomplished, past proceedings about the digital crime can be reconstructed, which forms the basis for a decision. The ultimate pronouncement is taken with the elucidation of the digital evidence by a group of persons other than the group performing the digital investigation. Digital investigation involved the development of theories and hypothesis by taking into consideration the events that make up the crime.

So the moral fiber of the digital investigation models [9] can be grouped as follows (as shown in Figure 2.2):

- Recognition of sources of digital evidence,

- Conservation of evidentiary digital data,

- Mining of evidentiary data from the digital media sources,

- Recording of digital evidence in the form of report.

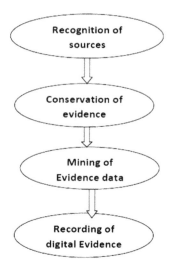

FIGURE 2.2   Stepladder of digital forensic investigation.

2.5.1 Recognition of Sources of Digital Evidence

This step of digital investigation can again be divided into two steps: first, the identification of the sources of digital data and second, the authentication of these sources as legally acceptable in the court of commandment. The sources of digital evidentiary data [7] may comprise various disk storage drives, memory cards, flash drives, Personal Digital Assistant or complete computer systems. When the sources are acknowledged, digital investigators must be able to distinguish appropriate and inappropriate data among the seized data since different crimes result in different types of digital evidence. Then, the media drives the start of the acquisition process followed by creating the exact replica copy for carrying out the inspection. The acquired media device is kept undisturbed to prevent fiddling authentic evidentiary data. The unnecessary media drives not related to the case investigation are exterminated from the digital investigation procedure.

2.5.2 Conservation of Evidentiary Digital Data

When the digital evidence has been recognized and recovered from the seized media drive, certain regulations, restrictions and constraints are to be followed for its conservation so that it can be demonstrated before the court of commandment [4,7]. The conservation of the evidentiary data decides its legal admissibility in the court of commandment. Conservation of evidentiary data should involve its segregation, security and protection to put off amendments. The integrity of the evidentiary data is checked by MD5 and SHA-1 algorithms. Anti-static bags are normally used to keep the seized media drives away from magnetic fields which justify its proper preservation.

2.5.3 Mining of Evidentiary Data from Digital Media Sources

Mining of evidentiary data from digital media sources is a tedious, time-consuming and complicated procedure. The type of mining of valuable data of interest is based on the digital crime case under investigation. The extraction of potential valuable data is unique and completely dependent on the procedure of retrieval and the technique of analysis being involved [7,10]. If the digital evidentiary data are directly available in the seized media drives, then the investigation takes less time. However, if the data is hidden or deleted, the time of investigation depends on the recovery of its deleted files. The media drive slack space may contain the remnants of the deleted or hidden files. Cybercrime investigation and examination involves the procedure for reconstructing the evidence data and proving it in a logical and scientific way. Depending on the digital crime case being inspected, the type of analysis procedure is chosen.

2.5.4 Recording of Digital Evidence in Form of Report

Documentation is a continuing process in the entire digital crime investigation. It involves the steps starting from evidence identification, its compilation, assessment and then documentation. This step includes noting down each and every step of the digital examination like how the digital crime case is seized; how the data is collected, conserved, recovered, reconstructed, formatted, organized and searched to find the potential digital evidence. The digital evidence must be accurate and written in a clearly understandable format [7,11]. It should be able to reconstruct the crime scene in order to defend against the digital crime being investigated.

2.6 DISCIPLINES OF DIGITAL FORENSICS

Digital forensics is mainly divided into three branches [2,3,8].

1. Computer forensics;

2. Network forensics;

3. Software forensics.

2.6.1 Computer Forensics

Computer forensics discipline is in the limelight because of the emerging acceleration of crimes due to unswerving use of computers in various forms such as entity of crime, a gadget used to commend an illegal activity or a warehouse of substantiation related to intrusive activity [12,13]. Computer forensics discipline can be dragged back to 1984 when the FBI laboratory and other law enforcement agencies developed programs to confirm computer proofs (Figure 2.3).

Computer forensic examination is a lingering and unwieldy process that needs forensic investigators' careful attention from months to years to obtain the potential data of interest that may exist on a suspected system [13].

According to the National Institute of Justice, the main goal of computer forensic examination is to trace the crime back to its origin and reconstruct the crime scene by well-approved methods for preservation, collection, validation, identification and interpretation of digital evidence [12].

The digital forensic examination is done to obtain the following:

1. Discovering all files, including deleted and concealed files, momentary or swap files on the subject system;

2. Finding the contents of shielded files;

3. Analyzing the unallocated space as well as slack space in the disk as it may contain the possible evidence;

4. Making a documentary report for the total steps of examination of the suspected system along with the possible pertinent files and exposed file data.

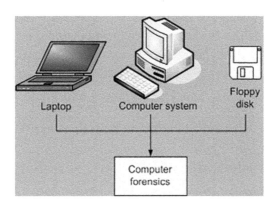

FIGURE 2.3 Computer forensics.

2.6.2 Network Forensics

The early 1990s marks the birth of the branch network or cyber forensics with an intention to prevent malicious hits into systems. Network forensics involves acquiring, storing and examining network audit trails with an intention to find the origin of security breaches or other information assurance problems [2] (Figure 2.4). This segment of digital forensics also covenants with extracting the potential valuable data by carrying out the postmortem analysis of network hits scenario. Such network threats include all types of cyber online attacks such as denial of service (DoS), distributed denial service attack, user-to-root and remote-to-local [2]. The network or cyber forensic branch covers the assortment of activities and diagnostic practices such as diagnosing the logs of intrusion detection systems (IDSs) [10], investigating the cyber traffic as well as network devices involved in the cyberattacks [2,4].

Standalone computers and networks involving interconnected computers agree on a common point that both the sources may contain potential legal digital evidence after an illegal attempt has been done. The router logs can be examined to get any suspected evidence about the malicious traffic. So the digital forensic analysis of the logs from different sources such as routers, switches, IDSs, firewalls, web servers and web proxies can help to maintain the security in standalone computer systems as well as in network or cyber forensics. Based on the need of digital crime investigation

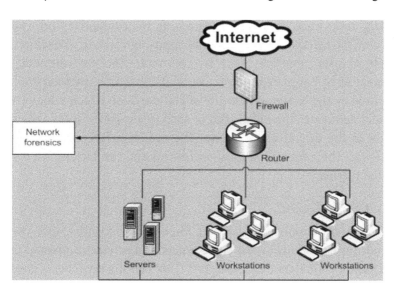

FIGURE 2.4   Network forensics.

and its type, the evidence is collected at the server level, proxy level or from several other sources. The happenings of the event along with their time of episode can be reviewed from web server logs. On the other hand, the accumulation of potential digital evidence is possible with the use of packet sniffers [3] for tracing inward network traffic to justify any type of digital crime.

2.6.3 Software Forensics

This branch of digital forensics covenants with code analysis to identify and categorize the author of malicious code [3]. The digital investigators in such type of crime investigation focus on recognition of biographer of malevolent code, unsolicited email, profiling and categorization.

2.7 DIGITAL CRIME INVESTIGATIVE TOOLS AND ITS OVERVIEW

The inspection and assessment of digital crimes are done by the digital forensic investigators using forensic investigation tools that help to conserve and repossess the potential evidence by maintaining its integrity and authenticity so that it can be further proved in the court of law. Investigation tools such as EnCase Toolkit [14], Forensic Toolkit [15], SafeBack Toolkit [16] and Storage Media Archival Recovery Toolkit (SMART) [17] are software packages and can be used for assembling and scrutinizing digital evidence. The digital investigation tools are used for specific tasks such as imaging, searching for evidentiary information and generating report. The tools hold opposing views in their functional graphical–user interface, that is, command-line environments that momentously boost exploratory work. Digital investigation tools are prepared by the National Institute of Standards and Technology (NIST) [8] that delineates the necessities of such investigative tools against the needs of the digital crime scene. The available forensic investigative tools with their functionalities, usefulness and limitations are demonstrated further.

2.7.1 EnCase Toolkit

The most commonly used digital forensic investigative tool used in various investigations by law enforcement and private companies is premeditated by Guidance Software [14]. This investigative tool is governed by the windows operating system mainly used to scrutinize, get hold of and prepare a statement on potential data of interest to be produced in the court of law. EnCase software creates a mirror image of the suspected hard drives so that the original evidence is not corrupted. The tool serves much functionality with a user-friendly graphical–user interface. The main attraction of the tool is to have a view of the suspected media prior to its replica creation. This feature of the investigative tool can help the digital investigator to determine whether the investigation is further required for the respective digital crime or not. A security key alternatively known as the dongle is required to operate the EnCase forensic software, which controls the accessibility to it. Every case in EnCase software is treated as a new case, leading to the suspected media drive imaging and its view. The media drive's acquisition is initiated for further investigation to find the potential evidence. The software has the capability to view all files, including hidden and deleted files. The authenticity is proved by using hash values generated by MD5 and SHA1 algorithms. EnCase provides different screens to display and review the data in different formats. A spreadsheet style format like a table is available, which depicts different pieces of information about the digital data, such as file name, file extension and type of file. The investigative tool also provides a facility to view the graphical images in thumbnail form so that it can enable the digital investigator to make access effortless and speedy. For an enlarged view of any suspected image from the thumbnail collection, the respective image can be clicked to see it at the lower section of the window screen. The tool also provides a calendar view from which information such as creation, accessed and modification dates of files can be collected. One can also customize the case-specific file activities. The report view of the investigative tool gives a full documentary report about the files and folders present in the suspected device. The documentary report also includes bit-level details such as total sectors, total clusters, size of the media, bookmarked graphical images and files, the operating system environment in the media drive system and the corresponding digital investigator conducting the investigation.

2.7.2 Forensic Toolkit

FTK investigative tool is cost-effective and beneficial forensic imaging software developed by Access Data Corporation [15]. It is mainly used for analyzing the emails. The operating system environment for FTK is windows, and it is less expensive than EnCase investigative tool. As the first important activity of any investigative tool is to create an authenticated copy of any media being accused, FTK has the software package to create a replica of hard disks and other media drives. FTK tool can make file formats as extensions such as .eo1, .smart, .aff and .raw. The various elements of FTK investigative tool are FTK Imager, the Registry spectator and the Known File Filter (KFF). FTK imager is responsible for creating the authenticated replica image of the accused media as well as sampling the total files in search of the evidence. Registry spectator inspects the registry files of the system under suspicion to have an overall information of files being present or modified in registry and passwords if at all used. KFF is mainly responsible for examining the authentication of the replica copy created for inspection by matching their hash values from a source database containing all hash values of known files. The analysis time is much more reduced with the self-identification of the file formats by the investigative tool. If the evidentiary information is found, then the total report starting from acquisition to evidence collection analysis is presented by the tool. FTK investigative tool is self-explanatory and comes with various options for checking the authenticity of the imaged media drive for examination by calculating MD5 and SHA-1 hash values. FTK comes with various functional windows such as case details overview window, Investigation Explorer window, Graphics, Evidence Search, Graphics, Email Analysis window and a special bookmark tab which gives quick access to all the important bookmarks already seen or solved digital crime cases.

The case details overview window narrates the files under inspection in a tabular format, which can be scrolled down to find an item of interest. Different files come with different sections as tabs. One can view the total files under that section by clicking on the respective tab. The Investigation Explorer window gives the exact structure of the hierarchy as narrated by the windows explorer in windows operating system. All the graphical images are deployed by the Graphics window in thumbnail form so that the investigator can select their evidentiary image for enlarged views. The area of expertise of this investigative tool lies with psychotherapy of email along with inbox messages to attachments as well as support for outlook express. The FTK tool comes with two powerful search approaches: live search and indexed search. The live search uses the technique of bit-by-bit comparison for the search items, and the indexed search involves dtsearch search engine [18], which works on the basis of suspected keyword search. Through a special bookmark window, the digital investigator can get a quick access to write additional comments to the evidentiary documentation report.

2.7.3 SafeBack Toolkit

SafeBack is a DOS-based digital investigative tool developed by Armor Forensics [16], mostly used by digital forensic investigators for computer safety measures worldwide. This investigative tool is capable of creating replica models of the accused media drives so that investigation can be done on the imaged drives without affecting the original copy. The functionalities of SafeBack is limited to imaging rather than searching or analyzing the files in the drives. SafeBack investigative tool makes use of the SHA-256 algorithm to guarantee the integrity of illustrations. The authentication codes generated by SHA-256 are stored along with data. In comparison with the other two investigative tools, SafeBack can be operated without a security key. SafeBack tool runs from the command-line prompt with a special command as Master. Exe.

2.7.4 Storage Media Archival Recovery Toolkit

SMART is governed by Linux operating system developed by ASR Data Acquisition and Analysis [17] mostly used by forensic investigative agencies, information security professionals and military people all over the world. In comparison with other investigative tools, SMART comes with user-friendly interface. It also combines much functionality for digital forensic investigation. SMART is an investigative tool that makes use of SHA-1 algorithm to check the authentication of the imaged media drives. It also provides the investigator an option to generate the hash codes using MD5 algorithm and cyclical redundancy check 32 algorithm [17]. In terms of functionality, SMART is only used for creating replica images with the help of bit-by-bit copy of the media drives under examination. The searching and reporting facility is also provided in this investigative tool. Security key is used to open the toolkit, and start using it for digital crime investigation.

This investigative tool also provides information on the seized hard drives such as the size of the seized device, the files and file formats present in the seized media device and the respective enduring data found in it. The investigative tool comes with various functional tabs like "Acquire", which helps in creating the exact replica of the media drives with the customized hashing algorithm per the user choice. SMART investigative tool comes with a various range of functionalities, including searching, filtering and hash cod generation and its matching with databases of hashes. The tool also has a graphic tab that enables the thumbnail representation of the graphical images. The images that form a part of the investigation process can be marked important. The Report generation tab helps in generating the detailed evidentiary document report and gives the option for its preview and adaptation. The evidentiary document report is generated in HTML format.

2.8 TAXONOMY OF DIGITAL CRIME INVESTIGATIVE TOOLS

All the digital investigative tools are developed keeping in mind the first requirement as creating the exact replica of the seized disk drives so that the original valuable data is not corrupted and the authenticity can be proved in the court of law with the generation of hash values. The generation of the hash codes helps in maintaining the accuracy and integrity of potential legal digital evidence in the imaged hard drives. The formation of the replica copy follows a bit-by-bit copy ensuring no amendment is done on the original copy. All the digital investigative tools except SafeBack are capable of executing analysis of files, its staging and respective case-specific keyword of interest search. The digital investigator has the privilege of looking at the files without altering it that can lend a hand in finding a case precise data. The presentation of the files includes all information such as the name of the file, file creation date and time and size of the file.

The taxonomy of digital investigative tools is possible based on the type of operating system being used by the investigative tool and the specific functionalities the tool provides (Figure 2.5). The categorization of the digital investigative tools is done with an aim to narrate the brief description of their current facilities and further find the limitations to deal with a growing need of computer fraud and cybercrime.

2.8.1 Functionalities of Digital Investigative Tool Can Be Grouped under

2.8.1.1 Replica of the Hard Drive

The first and foremost standard of digital forensic examination is to keep the original data untouched and rather requires the creation of the exact copy of the seized data. Replica creation is the process of making a mirror image by copying data sector-by-sector to obtain bitstream copy. Potential digital evidence is provided with an acquisition process along with MD5 hashing algorithm and SHA-1 algorithm to generate hash values for verification. Replica creation is a time-consuming process depending on the size of the media; then, it is further inspected for case-specific data.

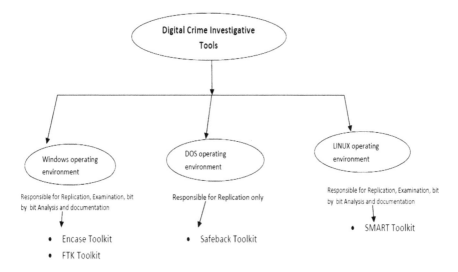

FIGURE 2.5   Taxonomy of digital crime investigative tools.

2.8.1.2 Investigational Analysis

After the collection of the data, analysis of the same has to be done for data interpretation and framing it in a constructive format. Data to draw concluding remarks about the evidentiary information is also important during this stage. Analysis of digital evidential data requires a variety of techniques such as searching keywords leading to finding out digital evidence. Keyword length should be kept short so that it can find out the word or strings in the slack or unallocated space [4,6–8]. Analysis technique also involves signature analysis that verifies the unique hex header signature for individual files. Analysis techniques include hash value generation and its matching, registry inspection, email examination and filtering.

2.8.1.3 Presentation

Analyzing the graphical images is a difficult task in a sort of digital investigation. The digital graphical images as well as video and audio files are not easily traceable in support of any digital crime that happened on the Internet. No software packages that can categorize the graphical images, audio files and video files from the seized media drives are also available. So the digital investigator has to view the content of the audio, video and image files manually by one, which is cumbersome, tedious and time-consuming task [2,3,8]. All digital investigative tools are equipped with presenting the files, which reduces the human activity and manual processing time. Viewing is the process of observing the files from the root level.

2.8.1.4 Documentary Reporting

Reporting is the important step of digital forensic exploration as it engrosses acquiring the resultant findings of digital crime investigation. Reporting is the representation of entire documentation, describing step-by-step investigational task like methods used to grab hold of, document, accumulate, conserve, recuperate, renovate, stride and look for key evidence [1,2]. The reports should be self-explanatory and traceable. It should specify all the files found directly present and the files that were deleted or that could complete the story of the digital crime incident. The report should document the odds and ends of all relevant digital evidence, as well as all corroborative information about the digital crime scene. The report should help the digital forensic investigator in finalizing the consequences of prosecution and should be accepted officially in the court of law.

2.9 BOUNDARIES AND COMMENDATIONS OF DIGITAL CRIME INVESTIGATIVE TOOLS

The present-day digital forensic investigative tools have many shortcomings with respect to complex digital crime incidents so this section of the chapter aims to outline and categorize the digital investigative tools based on their key advantages and functionalities, and put forward recommendations that can further be given future directions of research for empowering the existing investigative software tools to deal with modern-day digital crime. Forensic digital explorations are fetching more time and multifarious because voluminous data involved is more amplified [6,19–21]. Digital forensic investigations are depending on the currently available digital investigative tools to solve the crime cases because of the evolution of big data [19,20] in almost all fields. The visual presentation of the evidentiary data in tabular format by the digital investigative tools gets complicated and is misleading when the volume of the data to be analyzed becomes [21,22] data in terms of dimensionality, complexity and volume leading to confusion in locating precise information of concern. As the digital technology is being developed day-by-day, it is also being misused by the illegal people for nefarious gain. The size of the storage media is growing exponentially, making it impossible and impractical to do inspection for all the devices being seized. Therefore, it is necessary to apply various computer science methods and techniques so that search space can be slimed down into more easily managed areas. Trimming the investigation data makes it more sensible and rational to trace the valuable data, which could substantiate the potential digital evidence.

Currently existing digital investigative tools are suffering from the following limitations [3,7,21]:

- Reducing the redundancy present in the voluminous data,

- Recognizing the correspondences among data,

- Ascertaining the similarities and categorizing the data into groups,

- Making a simple and recognizable visual presentation of the data directly visible or hidden or deleted from the seized drives,

- Realizing patterns of interest that may end with the potential digital evidence.

The limitations and margins of the digital investigative tools may not tackle the growing dimensionality, complexity, volume, veracity and velocity of the data in this digital world. As profiling, tracking, tracing and seizing the cybercriminal are the important points in any type of digital investigation computational intelligence, fusion techniques to deal with volume, veracity and velocity of big data [6,19,20] enabling easy visualization should be developed and augmented with the basic digital investigative tools. Further enhancing the investigative tools to accommodate new problem-solving techniques and approaches will improve the competence and excellence of the digital forensic inquiry and research. The application of data fusion [23,24], data mining and machine learning algorithms [25] in the digital forensic investigation can tender numerous impending reimbursements for civilizing the eminence of judgments, plummeting human dispensation time and tumbling monetary costs. Future directions of research should be developing and discovering the augmentation packages for existing investigative tools to help the digital investigators to derive better conclusions so that digital information technology remains useful for the nation.

2.10 CONCLUSION

Computers play an integral role in the current world today as it is being habitually used by the people for day-to-day work. The Digital Information Technology Age has extensively enhanced our cerebral capabilities by providing superior information cargo space and scheming capacity. So people's mental power, reminiscence and assessment processes can be kept private and personal by not opening up to anyone as it is under the control of individual's brain but what we type into the computer system cannot be set aside as private. This principle makes it possible for the congregation of digital evidence. The assimilation of digital evidence is a challenging task because of the inscrutability of the computer systems afforded by cybercriminal to hide their identity. The major aim of digital forensics is to carry out digital investigations in order to trace the digital crime back to its source along with the perpetuation, permanence of digital evidence and intelligibility of the forensic investigation steps. Since the Internet is the largest network that interconnects each and every system worldwide, computer fraud and cybercrime can be committed from any point of the globe. To protect the sensitive information, it is not only necessary to take the protective measures but also necessary to be aware of such types of incidents. Regardless of many refined cynical procedures, information resources are still prone to frequent cyberattacks. So people all over the world should be well prepared to deal with such types of cyber threats. Though various investigative tools are offered on the market, their capabilities and limitations should be derived so that further research can be carried out to augment enhanced features along with it. In this chapter, the brief revision of digital crime investigative tools gives an impression of its current capabilities and describes the model steps to carry out crime investigation for collecting different types of digital evidence steadily. The main intention of the study is to derive a digital investigation model that can be used as assistance to existing evidence acquisition toolkits for supplying the offline admissible legal digital evidence.

REFERENCES

1. Association of Chief Police Officers, Good Practice Guide for Computer based Electronic Evidence, Available at: www.nhtcu.org, 2005.
2. Casey, E., *Digital Evidence and Computer Crime: Forensic Science, Computers and the Internet.* Academic Press, Cambridge, MA, 2004.
3. Casey, E., Network traffic as a source of evidence: Tool strengths, weaknesses, and future needs, *Digital Investigation*, 1(1), 28–43, 2004.
4. Palmer, G., A Road Map for Digital Forensic Research, Technical Report (DTR-T001-01) for Digital Forensic Research Workshop (DFRWS), New York, 2001.
5. Inman, K. and Rudin, N., *Principles and Practice of Criminalistics: The Profession of Forensic Science.* CRC Press, Boca Raton, FL, 2001.

6. Beebe, N. and Clark, J., Dealing with terabyte data sets in digital investigations. In: *Advances in Digital Forensics*, M. Pollitt and S. Shenoi (Eds.), pp. 3–16. Springer, Boston, MA, 2005.

7. Brezinski, D. and Killalea, T., Guidelines for Evidence Collection and Archiving, RFC3227, February 2002.

8. Carrier, B. and Spafford, E.H, Getting physical with the investigative process, *International Journal of Digital Evidence Fall 2003*, 2(2), 2003, 18–27.

9. Kruse II, W.G. and Heiser, J.G. *Computer Forensics: Incident Response Essentials*. Addison-Wesley, Boston, MA, 2002.

10. Palmer, G., *A Road Map for Digital Forensics Research-Report from the First Digital Forensics Research Workshop (DFRWS)*. Utica, New York, 2001.

11. Lipson, H., *Tracking and Tracing Cyber Attacks: Technical Challenges and Global Policy Issues*. CERT Coordination Center, Pittsburgh, PA, 2002.

12. National Institute of Standards and Technology (NIST), Computer Forensics Tool Testing (CFTT) project, www.cftt.nist.gov, 2005.

13. Wang, Y., Cannady, J. and Rosenbluth, J., Foundations of computer forensics: A technology for the fight against computer crime, *Computer Law and Security Report*, 21(2), 119–127, 2005.

14. Guidance Software, Inc., www.guidancesoftware.com, 2005.

15. Access Data Corporation, www.accessdata.com, 2005.

16. Armor Forensics, www.forensics-intl.com, 2006.

17. ASR Data Acquisition and Analysis, LLC, www.asrdata.com, 2005.

18. DtSearch Corporation, www.dtsearch.com, 2008.

19. AICPA, Big Data Listed as Top Issue Facing Forensic and Valuation Professionals in Next Two to Five Years: AICPA Survey, http://goo.gl/1BgdWB, 2014.

20. Davis, B., How Much Data We Create Daily, http://goo.gl/a0ImFT, 2013.

21. Zawoad, S. and Hasan, R., Digital forensics in the age of big data: Challenges, approaches, and opportunities, *ResearchGate*, 2015. doi: 10.1109/hpcc-css-icess.

22. Das, D., Shaw, U. and Medhi, S.P., Realizing digital forensics as a big data challenge. *4th International Conference on "Computing for Sustainable Global Development"*, New Delhi, India, 01–03 March, 2017.

23. Hall, D.L. and Llinas, J., An introduction to multi-sensor data fusion, *In Proceedings of The IEEE*, 85, 6–23, 1997.

24. Waltz, E. and Llinas, J., *Multisensor Data Fusion*. Artech House, Inc., Norwood, MA, 1990.

25. Han, J. and Kamber, M., *Data Mining: Concepts and Techniques*. Second edition. Elsevier, Amsterdam, 2005.

CHAPTER 3

Big Data Challenges and Hype Digital Forensic

A Review in Health Care Management

Anasuya Swain

College of Engineering Bhubaneswar

CONTENTS

3.1 INTRODUCTION

Big data is a popular term used in describing the vast growth and avail-ability of data both structured and unstructured (Sas 2000) with its massive usage of data sets acting as a helping aid towards the strategists, decision makers and experts of both service and manufacturing sectors. This ironical term is no doubt a gift due to its Internet technology-based feature and huge storage capacity for data collection and in-time availability data usage with clear visions by creating its importance in the field of health care. Big data application in health care helps to develop the various variables; many alternative solutions and answers to the dilemmatic questions at the emergency situation with valid inclusion are called catalysts. Health care sector also has the demand for big data due to its growth in the field of qualitative outcomes divided into eight dimensions: (i) predictive modeling for risk and resource usage, (ii) population management, (iii) product and service management, (iv) arising problems with its solutions, (v) storage of available literature, (vi) quality and valid decisions held, (vii) environmental reports and (viii) research applications. All of its importance is depending upon the analysis and interpretation of these big data.

3.2 BIG DATA FOR HEALTH CARE

Big data analysis for the successful medicine and hospitality management is emphasizing upon the big data's role in health care services. Murdoch and Datsky (2013) had done research on the field of health care with the application of big data. According to their findings, "Big data is an essential and effective tool for health care management but it has to adopt the developed technology to overcome the challenges that come with its own application.

Today, big data is developed as an indeed part of the medical science, and according to Rumsfed et al. (2016), "The big data has the need to provide quality and value-based services to the customers by availing data required with its analysis from the big data warehouse".

3.3 BIG DATA FOR HEALTH CARE STRATEGY MAKING

Big data analysis in health care sector is held with the proper procedure that has the need of a tool called data mining with the different dimensions of analysis such as (i) supervised, (ii) nonsupervised and (iii) semi-supervised learning (Murdoch & Datsky 2013, Rumsfed, Jayant & Mddore 2016, Raghupati & Raghupati 2014). Supervised learning is to predict a known output of target. Nonsupervised learning means the interpreter has only to do grouping/labeling. Semi-supervised learning means the balance performance and precision using small sets of labeled data. This analysis is itself a process that is held in different steps, and according to Lavindrasana et al. (2009) and Kaisler et al. (2013), big data analysis is performed in nine steps, which are as follows:

Step-1 Fixation of goal for health care sector with data mining application
  The fixation of the goal depends upon the business analyst's clear-cut business needs and its feasibility report. The analyst has to go for the feasibility test/situation analysis with the usage of tools like Political Economical Social Technological analysis and SWOT (Strength, Weakness, Opportunities and Threats) analysis through the available data. After the analysis of both the internal and external factors of the business need, a comparative analysis study has to be held and only the positive result is acceptable by the business analyst. But the business analysis of health care sector faces lots of obstacles to collect the data regarding their present and potential patient; however, it is now possible with the usage of big data. After data is drawn from the big data warehouse, it may be analyzed and compared for the positive result and health care business goal fixation.

Step-2 Data set selections
  The analyst has to collect various volumes of data from the available sources to get a rhythmic and effective decision. It also includes the various other events such as data loading, data integration, examination, querying, reporting and visualization of the

collected data from which valid data has to be gathered and grouped as data set after a proper verification.

Step-3 Data cleaning and preprocessing
This step is involved with the various events such as selection, cleaning, construction and formatting of data, to bring the data set to a proper format. This step takes the most amount of the time among the total steps of the big data analysis.

Step-4 Data rejection and projection
This step is an application of complex and intelligent methods to extract patterns from data such as task of association, classification, prediction, clustering and time-series analysis.

Step-5 Matching of the goal and data mining method
Here, the analyst has to make a match between the business need and reality available in the data set, which provides a clear understanding of the business need processes and its requirements. After clear-cut understanding, the business expert may go for the go-forward/not-go decision towards further.

Step-6 Choice of the algorithm and data pattern
Big data is available in different formats, and to make a unique and machine savvy format, the user has to go for the transformation of data in a mining procedure, which is held in two steps:

Data Mapping
It is the step to assigning elements of data from source base to destination to capture the transformation.

Code Generation
Creation of the actual transformation program is called code generation.

3.3.1 Pattern Developments

Here, the analyst has to go for the various techniques, which are applied to extract the various patterns, and has find their potential usage in the near or later future. The techniques generally have their applications in the following areas:

- Transforms task-relevant data into pattern,
- Decides the purpose of the model using classification/characterization.

3.3.2 Evaluation and Interpretation

The analyst here has to identify and select the best pattern which is knowledge based and can take interestedness measures. The pattern can be considered as interesting if it is potentially useful, is easily understandable by the general people and provides validity to the assumptions and confirmation towards the new data.

3.3.3 Result and Usage

The end result of the total process is information obtained from the data mining to be presented to the users. The users have to use different knowledge representation and visualization techniques to provide output towards the users.

The end result of the data analysis and data mining in the field of big data sometimes makes itself friend and sometimes develops as the foe by creating various challenges in the field of its usage.

3.4 OPPORTUNITY GENERATION AND BIG DATA IN HEALTH CARE SECTOR

Big data is developed as a very good friend for health care due to accessibility and usage of available big data information in clouding and other devices. Application of big data in health care administration describes the available information about the patient's medical record; current health situation, which is used to plan and fix the target patient participation in wellness; a smooth disease identification; and prescription management program. The medicine experts and doctors need the help of this tool for better management and understanding about the patients. This tool has a number of positive requirements and applications in the field of health care sector, which may be as follows:

3.4.1 Value Creation

Big data is a value-added tool towards the health care sector due to its number of characteristics, such as

   i. Transparency
      Open availability of health care data for initiation, development, closing and reopening of health care strategy and formation of health care system is a very good feature of big data called transparency. This feature helps to analyze various functions and maintain the quality, low cost and less time consumption to the market of health care.

ii. Supporting tool

This tool supports the health care facilitator for their interpretation and analysis in each and every location and the final decision about special events to meet their goal.

iii. Health care system segmentation

Business planner when goes for the new product development has the requirement of health care system division/segmentation thus assisted by the big data with the collection of various patients' information and health care unit segmentation in both micro and macro levels.

iv. Embedded sensors

Health care analysts/doctor has the requirement of the real-time information for their strategy making with the help of available analytical, applied data set and to collect the customer's response with the computer-assisted embedded sensors.

v. Cost reduction

Big data and cloud-based analyses bring cost reduction through the storage of a large amount of data, identification of proper procedure and feature for health care needs and development of proper management health care and hospitality sector with a reduction of expenditure in this field.

vi. Faster and better decision making

Analysis of new sources of data helps to analyze information immediately and make decisions easily and smartly, which are based on their learning.

vii. New products and services

New product development has the requirement of information about customer's need and their utility towards various features of the product and how it is possible to add value to this. The demand for the information need for customer environment analysis can be easily done through the help of big data analysis.

viii. Improved pricing

Big data helps to use health care intelligence tools and can give a clearer picture of where hospitality becomes more sophisticated by taking benefits that are available for its utility.

ix. Focus on local preferences

Small- to medium-scale industry has to focus upon the local environment for their catering service with their available and potential products. Big data helps to provide the local client's likes/dislikes and preferences even more. When the business gets to know the customer's preferences combined with a personal touch, the advantage would be gained over the competition.

x. Increased sales and loyalty

Big data analysis is a provision towards the exact patient's utility with the digital footprints such as online browsing and social channel postings.

xi. Hires and develops doctors and other facilitators

Available data regarding the various services provided by the health care unit with its lacuna and strength, future recruitment and selection will be held for the doctors and other facilitators, which will create friendly environment for the patient with efficient and eminent doctors to treat the patient with easy release from their disease and utility and value addition towards their money and create brand value for the particular hospital.

3.5 BIG DATA AND HEALTH CARE SECTOR IS MEETING NUMBER OF CHALLENGES

According to NewVantage Partners' Big Data Executive Survey 2017, only 48.4% of the total big data undertaken project had achieved their goal, which shows the challenges/issues in the field of big data. This helping aid has a number of issues in the field of capturing, processing, storage, analysis and visualization of data. Sometimes big data has its problem in the field of data analysis, development of the model solutions/result for the problem due to the faster-changing market and technology with the absentee of standard statistics and software. Big data in the field of health care sector is meeting a number of issues and challenges that can be retrieved through the help of data mining. The number of challenges and issues are as follows.

3.5.1 Volume

Big data, the name itself, is telling the huge amount of information whose size is beyond the ability of typical database software tools to capture, store, manage and analyze a large volume of data that is associated with the higher risk and difficulty for the analysis and interpretation to make a successful health care strategy. For this reason, one expert in the field of big data analysis (Ketchersid 2013) has rightly said, "Big data are necessary but not sufficient and can simply accumulate a large number of data set is of no of value", if the data cannot be analysed in a way that generates future insights that has its no usage for further usage.

3.5.2 Variety

Business environment analysis needs various kinds of data. In big data, a huge number of sources of data are available, whereas all the sources may not be valid and reliable. Sometimes unnecessary data lost the time and money and led to challenges with the creation of managerial bias in decision making.

3.5.3 Velocity and Variety

The flow of information and big data for different dimensions are not in a constant position; that is, they vary, which creates the challenges for the business analyst for its interpretation and analysis. Before one can go for any data interpretation, there is a requirement of checking data quality and availability. Sick and scared data leads to weak decisions.

3.5.4 Data Findings

It is tough to get the high-quality data from the vast collection of the web. Data analysts must take care to ensure the relevancy areas that are covered while the sampling is held and cannot avoid the challenges of data comprehensiveness. Sometimes data analysts collecting samples from the incomplete data may not perform a proper and right decision making.

3.5.5 Privacy

Sometimes the survey of personal life creates the barriers to collect the real and reliable data, whereas the big data usage can help to get it from the various data sets and sites for interpretation and development of the strategy without the intervention of the personal life of the people.

3.6 DIGITALIZED BIG DATA AND HEALTH CARE ISSUES

Data processing is the process of collecting the structured data for further analysis, that is, availability within spreadsheet or static software. Data set development leads to the analysis and interpretation of data, which should be tested by the expert in the field/area; then, it also faces the issues in the processing, which are as follows:

i. Scarce availability of practical benefits of big data analytics
   According to Joshi and Yesha (2012), "Big data contains both structured and unstructured data, whereas unstructured data contains the theme about the practical benefits from the health care are the data with natural language and hand written data, which creates the difficulty for integration, analysis and storage in a certain degree".

ii. Methodological issues such as data quality, data consistency, instability and various limitations are the validity of observations for analysis and legal issues.

iii. Lack of database upgrading and technology and computer literacy.

The big data with its limitations may not be ignored. By identifying the limitations, Wong et al. (2011) have with their research an argument that the complete case analysis consumes the time and reduces the data point to be effectively used to get the valid solution towards the arrived problem. High-dimensional data set, which is otherwise called a crude of dimensionality, is creating the problem in the application of big data. With the support of these ideas, Richard Bell Man had rightly given the statement, "There is difficulty in optimizing the data set". Alyass et al. (2015) after making the research have the positive impression for the big data usage in the field of data analysis because it can provide a logical interpretation and findings to the problem due to its various dimensions of data sets.

Big data in the hospitality management is suffering with the problem of bias in decision making, which is difficult to control. Here, Slobogean et al. (2015) have emphasized problem on the big data, and in their opinion, "Clinical studies, both observational and interventional, frequently lack the ability to provide reliable answers to their research questions because of inadequate sample size, underpowered studies are subject to multiple sources of bias may not represent the larger population in an regularly unable to detect differences between treatment groups most importantly, under powered studies an moreover lead to incorrect conclusions".

3.6.1 Effective Communication Safely Data Storage

Many patients do not want to share their personal data to avoid the disturbed personal life, and obstacles for the appointment, and get the insurance. All the legal provisions should be available for personal data protection right.

3.6.2 Availability of Data for General People

All the stored data/website-based data/cloud-based data may not be available on the website for all the people, which challenges the general people to access the information due to their internal survey and intellectual property.

3.6.3 Logical Data

Valid and reasonable data should be put in the data center. Manual data collected for health care sector may be with an error and with human bias. There should be certain instructions and guidelines for valid/scientific data about the human health care center and a regulating body to control the data.

3.6.4 Effective Communication of Health Care Data

Data communication between the data storage and data users should be effectively held by the development shared data platform with data sets and quality standards.

3.6.5 Data Capturing

Data has its need to be analyzed, which is collected according to the requirement to fulfill the objective of the analyst. The data that is collected may be categorical/numerical. Various sources have been taken to collect data such as technology personnel sensors in the environment, traffic cameras, satellites and recording devices. It may be held with the help of face-to-face interviews, reading documents and downloads of online sources. This stage contains the confusing facts and opinions that create a big problem in the data analysis step because effective analysis requires relevant facts to answer questions and test hypotheses but the fact from the various opinions may not be with the same structure or character.

3.6.5.1 Alignment of Data Sources

Captured and collected data has to be assigned in an organized way because collected data may be incomplete, contain duplicates or contain errors. To avoid these errors, there is the requirement of data cleansing as it is a process to prevent the error, match the records and identify the inaccuracy data. After data cleaning, it has to be analyzed through a variety of techniques, but inefficient cleaning leads to the wrong alignment of data with the wrong result. This alignment of data sources is suffering from the cognitive biases that can adversely affect the analysis. Individual persons may discredit information that does not support their views.

3.6.5.2 Algorithm of Data for Suitable Analysis

Various mathematical formulas are applied to the data in order to identify the relationship between the variables such as correlation and regression, but the user before going for the application of any algorithm should be clear about the particular formula with its application to avoid the negative result and precautionary action for the near future.

3.6.6 Understanding the Output and Accessibility towards the End Users

Analysis of data is held with a variety of numerical techniques with their results in a numerical format; however, audiences may not have such literacy with numbers.

Management of any organization with big data usage faces challenges such as security and privacy, governance and ethical standards and proper audit.

3.6.6.1 Privacy and Secrecy

Organization has to maintain certain secrecy for its competitive edge over other business units. When data mining is held for strategy making of that time, one alliance between cloud computing and big data image is held, which creates the problem such as data breaches, integrity, availability and backup.

3.6.6.2 Governance and Ethical Standards

Good governance of the organization has the requirement of cloud computing, and big data analysis is to provide the data at the time of demand, but lacks its dynamic feature due to its insufficient resource. Big data related to the production algorithm and the current algorithm is not available in the clouds, which creates the challenges for the management people for their effective governance. Algorithms used for the good governance also vary from person to person and vary with their results and reliability of their final result.

3.6.6.3 Proper Audit

A proper audit should be done by the management to test the reliability and relevancy of the data use in the field of big data. But sometimes web-based data hacking and its misuse may grow the power of the non-eligible individual and spoil the total business environment with the suffering of general people.

3.7 PRECAUTIONARY ATTEMPT FOR FUTURE BIG DATA HEALTH CARE

Various advantages of big data and assistance developed it into a helping aid and engross its importance. Importance and use of big data compel the various organizations and governments to go for precautionary attempts such as data storage, secrecy and web-based health care for genetic and chronic diseases. Now people can find the flood of data store construction and initiation because of huge data storage and information thereof for better hospitality and services in the field of public health observation, hospitality and pharmaceutical management and development. This storage is helping the doctor to identify in the field of different chronic diseases such as oncology, cardiology and numerology. Here, the data store has to make a register for each and every patient for the right time diagnosis along with the various types of treatments. All the developed countries have their data researchers and health officials using aggregated individual data to monitor global disease trends in real time (Zawoad & Hason 2015). Data storage helps to involve in research learning, training and development with its negative impact upon brand, policy, monetary scarcity and uncertainty.

3.7.1 Data Secrecy

Strategy making to develop a data survey is a very difficult task. Number of rules framework had developed for secrecy maintenance. EU framework for data protection in January 2012 has a view to modernize and harmonize data protection rules (Bhatta & Grover 2005). Health care sectors use big data to collect the patient stage information for secondary use. The secondary usage should not be the violation of secrecy and negative utilization of the individual data being collected.

3.7.2 Web-Based Health Care

Big data helps the doctors in involving in the field of effective disease management by taking preventive and cursive measures. It provides the sample with the health care management, medicinal usage and precautionary measures. Web-based health care facilitates the guidance, experience, advice and suggestions, symptoms of various diseases, remedy and management of medicine frame and its availability, accessibility, price discount from expert doctors, pharmaceuticals, patents, etc. This health care management can be held through the help of a complex algorithm and artificial intelligence of forensic science.

3.7.3 Genetically and Chronic Disease

Big data stores huge information about the genetically developed diseases and various chronic diseases with their symptoms, precautionary measures to be taken, medicines, cases and prescriptions; it has the requirement of a huge storage center. This raised problem in the field of data storage can be solved with the help of cloud computing by availing clouds for the company, organization and individual.

3.8 FORENSIC SCIENCE AND BIG DATA

Forensic science is a step-by-step action to control the illegal and unlawful and non-authentic events. When big data is suffering with the drastic challenge of ethics and secrecy of information, these forensic tools may be used as a good helping agent for the big data challenges by controlling the big data during the restricted time with the addition of best and vital forensic principles to be put in front of the court of law as the evidence.

Digital forensic is a tool which provides the proof that the status of occurrence of the event can genuinely be determined on the existence of valid digital evidence against that particular event (European Commission Report, 2019). Big data can be acquired from different foundations such as webpages, network/process logs and posts from social media documents, emails and data from innumerable sensors. Digital forensics is considered to have processes such as searching and recognizing a document and facts allied to the evidence; collecting evidence from cell phone, camera, etc; inspection, interpretation and correlation; maintaining integrity of the evidence, content exploitation via forensics linguistics and sentiment analysis techniques; and then disseminating the significance of the digital investigation admissible to the court (Chen et al. 2012).

3.9 TYPES OF DIGITAL FORENSICS

Digital forensics has been categorized into digital image forensics, mobile device forensics, volatile forensics, memory forensics, network forensics, antiforensics, application forensics, file system forensics, forensics frameworks and big data forensics.

3.9.1 Digital Image Forensics

Digital image forensics is a tool that provides the validity and authenticity of an image by identifying its history. This tool authenticates two problems:

- Determination of imaging device creating the image,
- Defined the footprints of counterfeit.

This tool provides its aid through the help of genomic analysis, predication, fraud analytics, predefined remote monitoring and patient profile analytics (Sinha, Hrispcsak & Makatou 2009).

Patil and Seshadri (2014) discuss how big data is being used in health care to lower cost while improving the care processes and delivery management. To eradicate the big data challenges in health care, big data forensics may be used, which is a tool that can help to identify, define, collect and store the digital evidence of the crime which is held digitally with its action of prevention and curative measures. Digital forensics tool will do its action function with its number of steps (Slobogean et al. 2015). Those steps involved in the digital forensic process are drawn data and its definitions and analysis, which are as follows.

3.9.2 Drawn Data for the Starting of a Process

The expert/examiner has to go for starting the process with the availability of huge data and making the system data duplicated once the data is duplicated to be tested. In this case, they did the data what they are searching for is called drawn data.

3.9.3 Big Data Analysis

3.9.3.1 Definition

The examiner has to test the data and has to find out the relevance; then the examiner files it into a different document test; if it is within the scope, work is taken forward/nevertheless stops.

3.9.3.2 Interpretation

Here, the examiner has to give a detailed description of the total data finding. This analysis will contain the involvement of an individual, place where it is held by an individual, the total time taken and the particular time data that is modified/deleted and accessed/copied. It is necessary that all the reports are to be written keeping a note of general layman understandings.

3.9.3.3 Big Data Framework

Experts/analysts are with their research to find out an appropriate framework by which the two areas scan to do their functions easily with blessings to the big data users. But still now, they are not successful.

Tahi and Iqbal (2015) used different techniques for the analysis of forensic data from large data, such as MapReduce, phylogenetic trees and blind source separation (Zaward & Hasn 2013), but with their result, they concluded that forensic science and big data make a challenge in the health care sector.

3.9.3.4 Forensic Tool Requirement for the Huge Data in Health Care

The inclusion of positive result towards effective management shows that there is a requirement of digital forensics science for the big data storage with its application effectively. Certain forensic science tools are used in the market for effective handling of big data security.

3.10 DIGITAL FORENSICS ANALYSIS TOOLS

Digital forensic analysis tools help to interpret the access, collect data to protect the evidence from the investigation and store for the evidence for further legal action. The tools are as follows.

3.10.1 AIR (Automated Image and Rest Store)

This is an open-source implication used to develop a forensic image. It characterizes the user-friendly and risk reducer of the "fat fingering".

3.10.2 Autopsy

It is a digital forensics tool for the usage of graphics and can recover the lost photos and videos from the cost device. It helps the corporate such as law enforcement professional, military agent professional and corporate detectives. This tool is very easy to use due to its certain characteristics such as

- Diversified action,

- Fast autopsy within a little,

- Cost-effective/time finds out.

3.10.3 Window Forensic Tool Chart

This chart is used for registration of windows with its evaluation. It works through filters and time stamps.

3.10.4 Digital Evidence and Forensic Tool Kit

This tool takes the curative measures to protect the fraud and crime. Here, the objective is to protect the system with safety and fraud-less devices such as the hard disks and pen drives. This tool is not only used for the health care sector but also has its more importance and usage to detect fraud crime in the general social life of human being.

3.10.5 EnCase

This forensic tool has its multiusage of time and pages of life with its various concepts.

3.10.6 Mail Examiner

This tool is used for the interpretation of the various emails. Here, the scope is speeded from the website of the email like personal mail.

3.10.7 FTK

This tool is used to find out the crime by interpreting the various data available in the various hard drives collected through the help of the FTK forensic tool.

3.10.8 Bulk Extractors

This tool collects the information from the output directory, which is in a hard disk format and is available with the information about credit cards, Internet mails, image and video, and telephone number.

3.10.9 Pre-Discover Forensic

This is a powerful tool that helps the professionals to find out the hidden data in the disk with its authenticity and security. It has the ability to restore the deleted files by utilizing its own pioneered technology.

3.10.10 CAINE

This tool is a software developed by the Linux, helps to provide a standard to the forensic to science tool and technology for the provision of safety data. It is a user-friendly forensic tool used for mobile network and data recovery forensic.

3.10.11 Xplico

It is a tool of forensic science used for software reconstruction of web-pages, images, files and cookies.

3.10.12 X-Ways Forensic

This tool develops an advanced environment for the collection of huge data resources with data recovery of deleted files with its very fast accessibility.

3.10.13 Bulk Extractor

This is a helpful element for the extraction of information from files and hard drives, and hence, it is a tool to perform a scan irrespective of the hierarchy of files.

3.10.14 Digital Forensics Framework

This is the tool used in open-source computer forensics platform built upon with programming for its simple usage and automation. This is a vital tool both for the experts and for the layman as the users for the data security access and to find the data-theft criminal activities.

3.10.15 Oxygen Forensics

This tool helps together the digital evidence from cloud services and mobile and collects the criminal activities and data theft and fraud by accessing these devices with the protection of the various personal data.

3.10.16 Internet Evidence Finder

This is designed for the forensic examiners with the help of the forensic laboratories, which has the power to access more than 2,000 Internet arti-facts and recover more data from more resources such as social network site, clouds, webmail and backups. It works very fast to make the quick search.

3.11 SOME OTHER INSTRUMENTS FOR BIG DATA CHALLENGE

Technological application with forensic science and big data can provide lots of solutions for big data challenges, and again, a rapid growth of tech-nology may change various kinds of techniques and methods for later future, which has its usability and importance today. These mostly used techniques are as follows:

1. MapReduce technique,

2. Decision tree,

3. Neural networks.

3.11.1 MapReduce Technique

MapReduce technique is applied at that time when the data is flown in parallel format, and there is no established correlation between the available data sets to find out the evidence about the forgery and illegal items. The analyzed data has to go for the logistic relation to reduce the horizon of the big data map. Reducing the map may create the established relation and work as a helping aid. Here, the analyzed data has to go for the implication of the algorithm to minimize the huge data set not by losing its originality.

3.11.2 Decision Tree

Decision tree is a technique/method developed by taking the fraud detection software to find a large statistical data set. In this field, it is difficult to suspect or identify the file with forgery or criminal activity among the availability of a huge data set. Still now, no automated system in this field of a decision tree is developed.

3.11.3 Neural Networks

Neural networks are suited for identifying difficult patterns from network forensics. Here, the network system has to take the training from a snapshot of the file to do further analysis. This is a very good instrument or tool for data set traffic control.

3.12 CONCLUSION

Big data is the best strategy-making tool that provides helping aid towards strategy making and provides services towards both the manufacturing and service sectors, especially the health care sector, which takes its advantage for its usage and its implementation for the growth, development and sustainability. The business analyst and strategist developer of all the sectors of the business world should go for the sage of big data set's help for their easy growth and sustainability in the market, but simultaneously they should implement forensic science tools and upgrade technology to take preventive measures in order to overcome the challenges of big data. Really, it can be concluded here that big data is a very good friend with the provision of value-added service and maximum consumer satisfaction towards the service sectors in general and health care sector in particular, but its challenges can be overcome with the leverage of updated technology and science-based forensic data tools.

REFERENCES

Alyass A., Turcotte M., & Myre D. 2015. From big data analysis to personalised medicine for all challenges and opportunities, *BMC Medical Genomics*, 8, 33.

Bhatta G.D. & Grover V. 2005. Types of information technology capabilities and their role in competitive advantage: An empirical study, *Journal of Management Information System*, 22(2), 253–277.

Chen P.Y., Chiang R., & Strong V. 2012. Business intelligence analytics from big data to big impact, *MIS Quarterly*, 6(4), 1165–1188.

European Commission 2019. Communication from the Commission: E – Health Action Plan 2012–2020. Com–lex.content/ENTXT/PDFI EUROPEAEDU/LEGAL?

Joshi K. & Yesha Y. 2012. Workshop on analytics for big data generated by health-care personalized medicine domain, *Proceedings of the 2012 and Conference of the Centre for Advanced Studies on Collaborative Research*, Toronto, Ontario, 267–269.

Kaisler, S., Armour F., Espinosa J.A., & Money W. 2013. Big data issues and challenges moving forward in system sciences (HISS), *Proceedings of the 46th Hawii International Conferences on System Sciences (HICC 2013)*, Grand Wailea, Maui, Hawaii, 995–1004.

Ketchersid T. 2013. Big data in nephrology: Friend or foe? *Blood Purification*, 36, 160–164.

Lavindrasana J., Cohen G., Depeersinge, A., Muller H., Meyer R., & Geeisssbuller A. 2009. Clinical data mining review, *Year Med-Inform*, 4(2), 121–1338.

Murdoch T.B. & Datsky A. 2013. The inevitable application of big data to health care, *JAMA*, 309, 1351–1352.

Patil, H.K. & Seshadri R. 2014. Big data security and privacy issues in the Health care sector, *Paper Presented at the2014 IEEE International Congress on Big Data*, Washington, DC.

Raghupati W. & Raghupati V. 2014. Big data analytics in health care: Promise and potential. *Health Information Science and Systems*, 2(1), 3.

Rumsfed J.S.S., Jayant K.E., & Mddore T.M. 2016. Big data analytics: Analytics to improve cardiovascular care: Promise and challenges, *Nature Reviews Cardiology*, 13, 350–359.

Sas N.D. 2000. What Is Big Data? Retrieved from: www.Sas.com?or_US?Insightsbigdata/whatisbigdata.html.

Sinha A., Hrispcsak, G., & Makatou M. 2009. Large datasets in Biomedicines a discussion of salient analytic issues, *Journal of the American Medical Informatics Association*, 16, 759–762.

Slobogean G.D., Giannnoudis P.V., Frihgen F., Fore M.L., Morshed S., & Bhandari M. 2015. Bigger data, bigger problems, *Journal of Orthopaedic Trauma*, 29, 43–46.

Tahir S. & Iqbal W. 2015. Big data an evolving concern for forensic investigators, *Paper Presented at the Anti-Cybercrime (ICACI), First International Conferences, New Delhi.*

Wong W.K., Boscrdin W.J., Postlthwaite A.E., & Furt D. 2011. Handling missing data issues in clinical trials for rheumatic diseases, *Contemplated Clinical Trial*, 32, 1–9.

Zaward, S. & Hasn, R. 2013. Cloud Forensic: A Meta Study of Changes, Approaches and Open Problems. Cornell University Library.

Zawoad, S. & Hason, R. 2015. Digital forensic is the age of big data challenges, approaches and opportunities. *Paper Presented at the High Performance Computing and Communication (ITPCE), 2015, IEE 7th International Symposium on Cyber Safety and Security (CSS) 2015, New Jersey.*

CHAPTER 4

Hadoop Internals and Big Data Evidence

Bhagirathi Nayak

Sri Sri University

CONTENTS

4.1 HADOOP INTERNALS

Hadoop is presently the most broadly embraced Big Data stage, with a different environment of uses and information hotspots for criminological proof. As an Apache Foundation framework solution, Hadoop has been created and tried in endeavor frameworks as a Big Data arrangement. Hadoop is for all intents and purposes synonymous with Big Data and has turned into the true standard in the business and industry.

As a new Big Data solution, Hadoop has encountered a high appropriation rate by numerous sorts of associations and clients. Created by Yahoo! In the mid-2000s, Hadoop has discharged to the Apache Foundation as one of the main significant open-source Big Data structures. Hadoop is intended to empower the appropriate handling of huge, complex informational indexes over clustered computers. Hadoop's conveyed design and open-source environment of programming bundles make it perfect for speed and adaptability. Hadoop's selection by enormous-scale innovation organizations is well advanced, and numerous kinds of associations and clients have come to receive Hadoop also. Hadoop incorporates logical analysts, medicinal services organizations and information-driven advertising firms. Seeing how Hadoop functions and how to perform criminology on Hadoop empowers agents to apply that comprehension equivalent to other Big Data arrangements, for example, PyTables.

Performing Big Data criminological examinations requires learning of Hadoop's internals and also Hadoop's engineering. Similarly, as knowing how the NTFS file system functions are significant for performing legal sciences in Windows, knowing the layers inside a Hadoop arrangement is indispensable for appropriately recognizing, gathering and breaking down-proof in Hadoop. In addition, Hadoop is quickly changing new programming bundles that are being included and refreshes. Hadoop is being connected all the time. It is essential to have a basic learning of Hadoop's engineering and how its capacities will empower an examiner to perform criminology on Hadoop as it keeps on extending and developing.

With its own file system, databases and application layers, Hadoop can store information (i.e., proof) in different structures and in various areas. Hadoop's multilayer architecture keeps running over the host-working framework, which means that proof may be required to be gathered from the host-working framework or from inside the Hadoop environment. Evidence can reside in every one of the layers. This may require performing scientific gathering and investigation in a way explicit to each layer.

This section investigates how Hadoop functions. The accompanying points are shrouded in detail: Hadoop's design, records and information input/output (I/O). This section gives a comprehension of the specialized underpinnings of Hadoop. The key segments of the Hadoop measurable proof biological system are mapped out, and finding a proof inside a

Hadoop arrangement is secured. Finally, it concludes with guidelines on the most proficient method to set up and run LightHadoop and Amazon Web Services, which are presented as the Hadoop occasions that fill in as the reason for the models used in this book. On the off chance that you are keen on performing criminological examinations, you ought to adhere to the guidelines on the most proficient method to introduce LightHadoop and set up an Amazon Web Administrations example towards the finish of this section. These frameworks are important to pursue the models introduced all through this book.

4.2 THE HADOOP ARCHITECTURES

Hadoop is a solid framework for imparted stockpiling and examination to a rich environment of layered arrangements and devices for Big Data (Figure 4.1). Hadoop is based on the ideas of dispersion for capacity and registering. It is a cross-stage, Java-based arrangement. Hadoop can keep running on a wide exhibit of various working frameworks, for example, Linux and Windows, since it is worked in Java, a stage nonpartisan language. Hadoop itself is a layer that sits over the host-working framework. Hadoop's center functionalities are likewise implicit Java and can be kept running as independent procedures. With its own file system and set of center functionalities, Hadoop fills in as its own unique stage layer; it can be gotten to and run primarily free of the host-working framework.

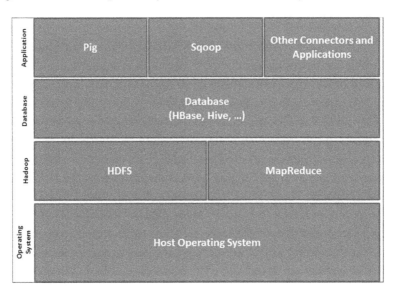

FIGURE 4.1   The Hadoop architecture layers. (https://subscription.packtpub.com.)

The Hadoop layers are an abstraction for how the various components are organized and the relationship between the other components. The following are the various Hadoop layers:

The operating system layer: The primary layer is the operating system on the host machine. Hadoop is installed over the working framework and runs the equivalent of the host operating system (for instance, Windows or, on the other hand, Linux).

The Hadoop layer: This is the base installation of Hadoop, which incorporates the record framework and MapReduce mechanisms.

The DBMS (Data Base Management System) layer: On top of Hadoop, the different Hadoop DBMS and related applications are introduced. Normally, Hadoop establishments incorporate information warehousing or database bundle, for example, Hive or HBase.

The application layer: The application layer is the top layer, which incorporates the instruments that give information to the executives, investigation and different abilities. A few apparatuses, for example, Pig, can collaborate straightforwardly with the working framework and Hadoop layers. Different apparatuses just communicate with the database layer or other application-layer instruments.

4.2.1 The Components of Hadoop

The Hadoop layer is the most significant layer in seeing how Hadoop functions; furthermore, it is not quite the same as a database management system or other large-scale data processing engines. This layer contains the center's Hadoop components, the Hadoop Distributed File System (HDFS) and MapReduce functions. These components structure the key capacities for managing the storage and analysis of data. A Master Node computer manages the delivery and controls Slave Node machines also for document storage and data analysis. Figure 4.2 demonstrates how the Master Node controls the Slave Node in the Hadoop layer for MapRed and HDFS.

Hadoop uses HDFS to logically store data for its application. HDFS is designed to store a distributed fashion of data on commodity storage hardware. The directory NameNode manages the data storage and management activities across each DataNode. The NameNode file dynamically stores and replicates the data in several blocks (default 64 or 128 MB) across the

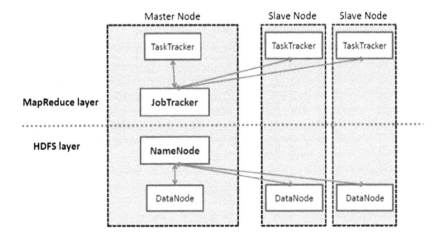

FIGURE 4.2   The Hadoop distributed process. (www.dezyre.com/.)

specific DataNode when data is stored in Hadoop. This is done to ensure high availability and tolerance for faults.

MapReduce is a key concept and application for the storage of information by Hadoop. MapReduce allows large jobs to be divided into Map. Tools use Hadoop's distributed computing platform. The Map is filtering and sorting operation, while the Reduce is a summary operation, for example, summation or counting. It is possible to divide a single request into Map and Reduce procedures with a Master Node assigning the tasks to each Slave Node. The Slave Node performs its discrete tasks, transmits the reports for analysis collection and reports back to the Master Node.

Figure 4.3 shows an example of how a MapReduce function works.

The first step of MapReduce is to run the initial input data with a Map. It generates information subsets that can be distributed for storage to one or more nodes. In this example, the input data consists of information, with each node receiving information about one widget. Each node receiving a record performs a record operation. The nodes will calculate the total information. Ultimately, for all widgets, shuffle and then reduce the information for output.

We can write and execute MapReduce programs in a number of different ways. Next, the org.apache.hadoop can be used to write programs natively in Java. The library of the mapred. uses a Java compiler; a MapReduce program is compiled and then run using the Java runtime in Hadoop. Additional Hadoop packages provide MapReduce abstractions that can

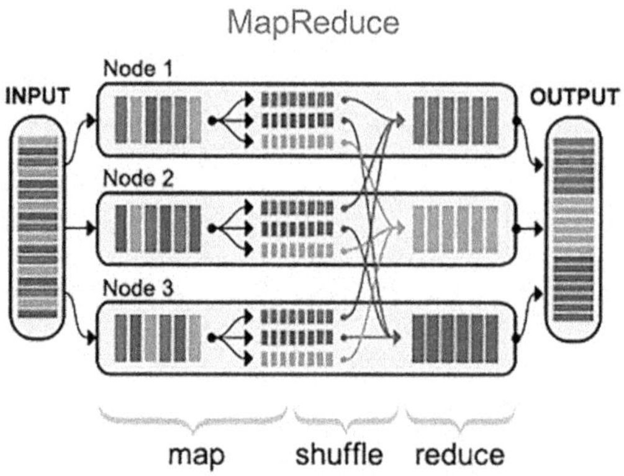

FIGURE 4.3 The Hadoop MapReduce process. (www.computerhope.com/jargon/m/mapreduce.jpg.)

TABLE 4.1   Data Format of MapReduce

Tools	Description
Hive	This is a data warehouse that provides data in HDFS with SQL-like access
HBase	This is a column-based data warehouse to perform operations over large data sets at high speed
Pig	This is the framework to use its own scripting language to execute MapReduce on HDFS files
Scoop	This is a method for transferring data to and from relational database systems
Flume	It harvests, aggregates and transfers in and out of Hadoop large amounts of log data

implement Map and Reduce without Java (e.g., Pig) being used. The layers above the Hadoop layer are the system and resource management add-on features. Such layers store, extract, transform and analyze data. Examples of resources used in these layers are given in Table 4.1.

4.3 THE HADOOP DISTRIBUTED FILE SYSTEM

HDFS is the file system that Hadoop mainly uses. It is an abstract file system layer that stores data to enable cross-platform functionality in its own format. The real data space resides in the file system of the host operating system. In Hadoop blocks, however, the logical files are stored; they are not necessarily directly accessible from the host operating system as would be a file stored in the host-operating system. The aim of HDFS is to

- Maintain the storage of data on a cluster,

- Maintain storage delivery by NameNode and DataNode,

- Segment files into DataNode blocks,

- Provide access to the information blocks content.

HDFS is just one of more than ten file systems that Hadoop can implement. Although HDFS is the most common file system in Hadoop and the one discussed in this book, researchers should be aware that a cluster in Hadoop could use a different file system. Kosmos, Amazon S3 and the local file system are several examples of other Hadoop file systems. Data will be imported into HDFS and stored for distributed storage in blocks. It is possible to import files and data into HDFS in a number of ways, but all data stored in HDFS is separated into a set of frames. The blocks are only separated by volume. A file contains record information, and if that record covers a block size boundary, the splits may occur within an individual document. By definition, blocks are 64 or 128 MB in size, but a system administrator may adjust the size to a different number. Hadoop is intended to work with data terabytes and petabytes. The metadata is stored centrally on a database for each file, so Hadoop cannot afford to store the metadata in 4 KB data frames. Therefore, Hadoop'.

Hadoop is stored in a number of DataNode files after the data is broken. The replication level is set to three DataNode files per block by default, but a system administrator can also adjust that setting. Mapping information shows the location of the data blocks and other metadata in the NameNode located in the Master Node. Figure 4.4 illustrates this process.

NameNode is a single failure point. While information about DataNode is stored in multiple locations, information about NameNode resides only in one machine unless a secondary NameNode is set up for redundancy.

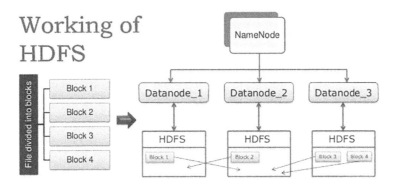

FIGURE 4.4 HDFS data block distribution. (https://factspan.com/cms/wp-content/uploads/2019/08/HDFS-working.jpg.)

Data are logically stored in HDFS and can be accessed in any other file system via HDFS just like a file. A number of DataNode files can be stored in data blocks, but the files still retain their file names and can be accessed in a number of ways. NameNode stores the information needed to find a file name that defines where the various blocks that compose the file reside and provide security at the file level. When a file request is made in HDFS, Hadoop retrieves data blocks and provides access to the data as a file.

4.4 DATA ANALYSIS TOOLS

Hadoop is designed for large quantities of data being processed and analyzed. The Hadoop research software ecosystem is large and complex. There are many different methods that can be used depending on the type of analysis. The toolset of the Apache Foundation has a number of standard choices such as Hive, HBase and Pig, but other open sources and commercial implementations have been developed using the HDFS and MapReduce functionality of Hadoop to meet different analytical requirements. For example, the Impala database of Cloudera runs on Hadoop, but it is not part of the application suite of the Apache Foundation.

To define and properly collect data, it is important to know that data analysis tools are used in a Hadoop cluster. Many tools for data analysis store data in compressed files and may provide simpler data collection methods. Other tools can read data directly from files stored in HDFS, but when analyzing the data later, the scripts used for the tool can provide useful information. This section explores the three most frequently used tools for data analysis, namely, Hadoop Hive, HBase and Pig.

4.4.1 Hive

This is a data warehouse that provides data in HDFS with SQL-like access. A hive is an infrastructure tool for data warehouse processing of structured data in Hadoop. To summarize Big Data, it resides on top of Hadoop and makes it easy to query and analyze.

This is a short tutorial on using HDFS Apache Hive HiveQL. This tutorial will be your first step towards becoming a good developer of Hadoop with Hive.

Hive is not

- A relational database,
- A design for OnLine Transaction Processing (OLTP),
- A language for real-time queries and row-level updates.

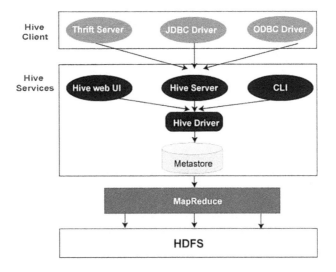

FIGURE 4.5 Hive architecture. (https://static.javatpoint.com/hadooppages/ images/hive-architecture.jpg.)

Features of Hive

- It stores schema in a database and processed data into HDFS;
- It is designed for OLAP;
- It provides SQL-type language for querying called HiveQL or HQL;
- It is familiar, fast, scalable and extensible.

Figure 4.5 portrays Hive architecture.

4.4.2 HBase

This is a data warehouse focused on columns for high-speed operations execution over data sets. HBase is a distributed database that is column-oriented and built on top of the Hadoop file system. It is an open-source project that can be horizontally scaled. HBase is Google's big table-like software model designed to provide easy random access to huge quantities of structured data. It leverages the fault tolerance of the Hadoop file system. It is part of the Hadoop ecosystem that provides real-time read/write random access to data in the Hadoop file system.

The data can be stored either directly or via HBase in HDFS (Figure 4.6). Data users' read/access data randomly used HBase in HDFS. HBase is located at the top of the Hadoop file system, which enables read and write access.

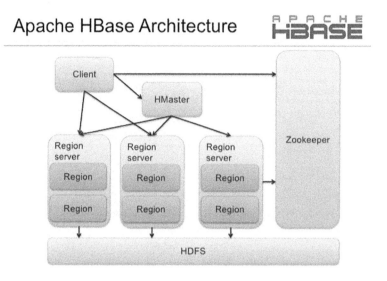

FIGURE 4.6 HBase architecture. (http://a4academics.com/images/hadoop/ HBase-Architecture.jpg.)

HBase is an open-source, non-relational, column-oriented distributed database built on top of HDFS as part of the Apache Software Foundation for faster read/write operations on large data sets. This offers faster data recovery due to indexing and transactions for any search query. It also offers configurable tables sharding, linear/modular scalability, natural search for language and real-time queries.

4.4.3 Pig

This is the framework to use its own scripting language to execute MapReduce on HDFS files. Apache Pig generally works on top of Hadoop. It is an analytical tool that analyzes massive Hadoop file system data sets. We must first load the data into Apache Pig to analyze data using Apache Pig. This chapter describes how data can be loaded from HDFS to Apache Pig.

Pig Latin is the language used to analyze data using Pig in Hadoop. It is a language of high-level data processing that provides a rich collection of data types and operators to perform different data processing operations. Programmers need to write a Pig script using the Pig Latin language and execute it using any of the execution mechanisms (Grunt Shell, UDFs, Embedded) to perform specific task programs using Pig. After execution, to produce the desired output, these scripts will go through a series of transformations implemented by the Pig Framework.

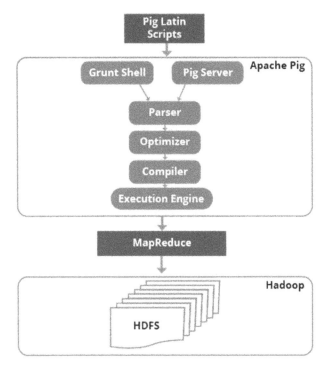

FIGURE 4.7 Pig architecture. (https://www.tutorialspoint.com/apache_pig/images/apache_pig_architecture.jpg.)

Internally, Apache Pig transforms these scripts into a series of MapReduce jobs, making it easy for the programmer to work. The architect of Apache Pig is shown in Figure 4.7.

4.4.4 Scoop

Big Data is the standard software management system, that is, the integration of applications with relational databases using RDBMS. This RDBMS-generated Big Data is stored in the context of the relational database on relational database servers. When the Big Data storage and analyzers such as MapReduce, Hive, HBase, Cassandra and Pig. from the Hadoop ecosystem came into the picture, they needed a medium to connect with the relational database servers to import and export the Big Data that resides within them.

Here, in the Hadoop ecosystem, Sqoop occupies a position to provide feasible communication between the relational database server and Hadoop's HDFS. This is a method for transferring data to and from relational database systems. Sqoop is a data transfer tool between Hadoop

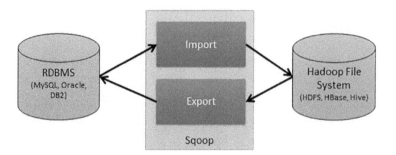

FIGURE 4.8 Scoop architecture. (https://www.hdfstutorial.com/wp-content/uploads/2016/07/Sqoop-architecture.png.)

and relational database servers. It is used to import data from relational databases such as MySQL and Oracle to Hadoop HDFS, and export from the Hadoop file system to relational databases (Figure 4.8). This is a brief tutorial explaining how Sqoop can be used in the ecosystem of Hadoop. Sqoop is a method of data transfer between Hadoop and relational database servers. The Apache Software Foundation supports it.

4.4.5 Flume

Flume is a standard, quick, scalable, versatile and extensible platform for data ingestion into Hadoop from different data producers (web servers). We will use a clear and illustrative example in this tutorial to explain Apache Flume's fundamentals and how to use it in reality. Apache Flume is a tool/service/information ingestion system for aggregating and transporting large amounts of streaming data from various sources to a centralized data store, such as log files. A flume is a tool that can be programmed, distributed and highly reliable. It is primarily designed to copy data streaming from various web servers to HDFS. Figure 4.9 shows the structure of the flume.

4.5 LOCATING SOURCES OF EVIDENCE

It is critical to success in locating and thoroughly gathering relevant evidence in the early stages of an investigation. At a minimum, an inaccurate compilation of facts can result in an awkward and difficult process of remedial measures as well as wasted time. At worst, it will result in inaccurate compilation operating with the wrong data set. In the latter situation, it is possible to foresee court penalties that have failed causes

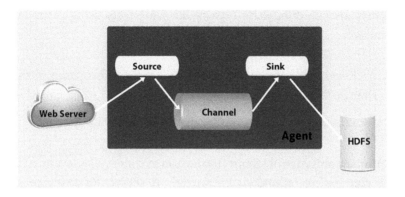

FIGURE 4.9 Flume architecture. (https://d2h0cx97tjks2p.cloudfront.net/blogs/wp-content/uploads/sites/2/2018/02/Flume-architecture-2-1.png.)

and damaged reputations. This chapter provides guidance for the classification of all relevant data so that these circumstances do not arise.

It is a complex process to classify facts. This process includes reviewing a set of potential proof causes and deciding that bases warrant compilation. Data are seldom well structured or reported in the structures of any organization. Researchers will need to take a set of study criteria and decide what information to collect. The following steps are needed:

- Analysis of device and software documentation properly,

- Position of backup and non-centralized repositories of information,

- Interviews with employees,

- Preview of the data.

The procedure of defining Big Data evidence is complicated by the vast volume of data, scattered file systems, multiple data forms and evidence-based forms possible for significant redundancy. Big Data approaches are also different in that proof can be collected in various layers within Hadoop. Proof can take on multiple forms from Hadoop Internals and Architecture. Multiple layers were analyzed to properly identify the proof in Hadoop. While all the data may be in the HDFS, the structure may vary in a Hadoop framework, the HBase; or the data may be extracted more easily via an application of Pig or Sqoop, which is a suitable format via HDFS.

It may also be difficult to classify Big Data facts using redundancies caused by

- Archived applications that may have stored information in the Big Data process beforehand,

- Systems entering and receiving data from Big Data systems.

The primary objective of identifying facts is to collect all relevant evidence while eliminating redundant knowledge. A server, for instance, could move all information about sales into a Hadoop framework. Hadoop's sales database and sales data may be an exact match or inconsistencies that occur as a consequence of either or both systems updating the information after the move. If the data is the same, it would be wasteful to obtain them, resulting in unnecessary time and resources. A forensic investigator needs to understand the correct source from which to gather the evidence or whether to catch all sources.

Outsiders looking at the data needs of an organization may presume that it is as easy to define information as to tell many individuals where the data resides. In reality, for a number of possible reasons, the process is much more complicated, which are as follows:

- The company is big and no one knows where all data is stored and what the information value is.

- The company can be an adverse party and cannot be trusted in providing reliable data information.

- The company is split into business units without two business units recognizing the data stored by the other.

The method then unifies knowledge directly and produces compelling sales-driven analyses. In fact, a researcher will probably find that the Big Data marketing system actually consists of a wider set of data from within and outside the company. Desktops or notebooks for sales workers may have a range of tablets, along with some older versions of backup tapes or shared folders on file servers. A new 2-year-old Salesforce database that happens is outdated and simply replaces a previous database that employees have custom-developed and used. A Hadoop instance running HBase for analysis receives from social media, Salesforce server and sales reports a filtered set of data from feeds. Different teams have to manage all these data sources, and a number of steps to isolate the relevant information are involved in determining how to obtain this information.

For large or even mid-sized enterprises, the dilemma is much more complex than the pharmaceutical sales business case. In-depth interviews with key business owners and staff can take weeks to rapidly create a map of each data source and the contents of those systems. Some organizations may have their own databases or Big Data systems that may or may not be housed in a centralized repository. For such phones, backups can be found anywhere. Knowledge retention policies will vary from department to department and most likely from the technique. Data warehouses and other aggregates can contain important information not revealed by routine interviews with workers.

Big Data proof can be mixed with non-Big Data proof. E-mail, paper files and other information can be extremely valuable when carrying out an investigation. The process for identifying Big Data is very similar to the process for identifying other evidence, so in combination with other evidence, it is possible to perform the identification process outlined in this book. An important factor for investigators to bear in mind is whether Big Data should be obtained from other non-Big Data systems, whether it is appropriate or whether the same information can be gathered more easily.

4.5.1 The Data Collection

It is an iterative process to find the data sources to be collected. This process includes the collection of data requirements, the identification of which systems are available, the determination of which systems contain data that meet the requirements, and the assessment of the feasibility of collection of data in the relevant systems. Figure 4.10 shows the top-down method in detail.

Detailing the data collection process involves assimilating all information from client interviews and gathering documents to form a detailed plan and set of data collection criteria. The specifications should be in a clear and straightforward language that anyone can understand. Complex specifications in highly technical or legal language may lead to a misunderstanding between the researcher and the data collector. Make sure to state the relevant facts about the data types that need to be

FIGURE 4.10   Top-down method.

obtained, and clearly mention all the requirements and criteria for supporting documentation.

If a system contains semi-useful data, it is necessary to answer several questions, which are as follows:

- Is the semi-useful data source a bridge between the required data sources, or is it used to fill a gap or fix a data deficiency in the data needed?

- Does the required source of data contain information that can address all the facts? If not, are any of the remaining facts addressed by the semi-useful data source?

- Is the effort needed to collect semi-useful data small, and is the amount of information manageable?

If the answer to any of these questions is yes, the investigator must consider including in the data collection the semi-useful data. The explanations are as follows:

- The semi-useful data play a secondary role in allowing the research with the necessary data to be carried out;

- The semi-useful data is actually necessary;

- The effect of data collection is small, and the inclusion of the data does not hurt.

Any information found non-relevant during the data collection process should be carefully considered by the investigator. During the initial stages, the danger of not collecting data is that there will be no second chance of collecting it. The data may be subsequently deleted or changed, and there may not be another opportunity to obtain the information. At a later stage, the timing of a second data collection could hamper research.

Consider whether a data source is redundant when determining the following:

- Is the information to be obtained completely redundant to another data source?

- Which information is included in the data?

- Will the data still exist at a later date in its current form?

The investigator will report the answers to these questions even if the data source is redundant. Ignoring a source of data at a later stage can require justification. If any questions are asked at a later stage, recording the reasons when the data is first made available will allow the investigator to provide a clear answer.

4.5.2 Structured and Unstructured Data

Big Data included structured and unstructured data principles. However, when collecting Big Data, the line between the two may become extremely blurred. It is possible to store both structured and unstructured data in a Big Data system. The investigator must understand the difference between these forms and whether it is necessary to collect data in a structured or unstructured format. Structured data provides the benefit of the simpler analysis, but it can be slower and provide more material to capture unstructured data in its original form.

Big Data systems can contain multiple forms of data. It is possible to import, store and query unstructured text files in Hadoop. This unstructured data can then be converted and combined with other data sources in a structured form. The investigator should be aware of the different data structures to be identified and collected.

Under the umbrella of structured data analysis in later stages, there are several types of unstructured or semi-structured data. For example, for accounting purposes, users at a business must maintain a collection of restricted or markup files. While these files are considered technically unstructured, they contain structured data. It would not be wise to ignore these files merely because they have been stored in an unstructured file format. Alternatively, it is important to compile the spreadsheets and then convert them into a standardized format for review. Table 4.2 displays the data format in a delimited file.

Unstructured data do not have the same rules and composition restrictions that structured data have. This lack of rigidity and structure allows data to be stored and presented in varied ways. Some of the most common forms of unstructured data include the following:

- E-mail,
- Presentation documents,
- Video and audio files,
- Textual documents (e.g., MS Word documents and PDF files),
- Graphics files,
- Executable binary files (e.g., Windows.EXE files).

Many types of these files, including unstructured or semi-structured data, can contain structured information. Client interviews will allow the investigator to decide whether these files should be collected and whether

TABLE 4.2   Data Format

CustNum	Name	Address 1	City	State	Zip	Notes
1000011	John Doe	123 Mani Street	Centreville	VA	55555	Paid on time
1000012	Jane Doe	123 Mani Street	Centreville	VA	55555	Delinquent follow-up required
1000013	Joe Doe	456 Center Road	Anytown	GA	55554	N/A
1000014	Jill Doe	456 Center Road	Anytown	GA	55554	Call 5551230002

a structured or unstructured type of data collection method exists. Unstructured text files, for instance, can be stored in an HDFS, but this information can be collected via Hive or Sqoop in a structured form. The investigator must also decide how to check the collected data, which is simpler when gathering the whole unstructured archive.

4.5.3 Data Collection Types

It is possible to make two primary categories of data collections. Next, the investigator must conduct the data collection. In this case, by accessing the source systems, the investigator conducts the forensic compilation and collects the data for offline analysis. Instead, the prosecutor can ask the device owner or third party to collect the data in some situations, such as civil litigation. In such situations, in the collection process, the investigator can supervise, advise or simply be a passive participant.

Investigation criteria determine what alternative is selected. Collections made by the investigator have the advantage of being correctly performed and verifiable. The investigator knows what data to collect and uses best practices to perform the collection. The set is less likely to be challenged because the investigator is impartial. A selection led by a company or by a third party has the benefits of being potentially cheaper and less harmful to the organization. The drawbacks are that the collection may not be carried out correctly, data may be altered accidentally or intentionally and the collection may not be carried out as quickly as possible. The ultimate arbiter deciding who should conduct the collection is the individual investigation criteria such as investigation problems, time constraints and cost factors.

4.6 THE CHAIN OF CUSTODY DOCUMENTATION

It is necessary to establish the chain of custody documentation as soon as evidence is collected. If a collection is carried out by in-house staff or a third party, the person performing the collection and anyone taking possession of the evidence must fill out the chain of custody forms. The chain of custody documentation is a chronological history showing who owned the evidence. In both criminal and civil cases, this is necessary to establish who had access to the evidence and who might have manipulated the evidence. Each time the information is shared between two parties, when the transition happened and who was involved; the custody data chain should be updated to record. Figure 4.11 shows a custody record review chain.

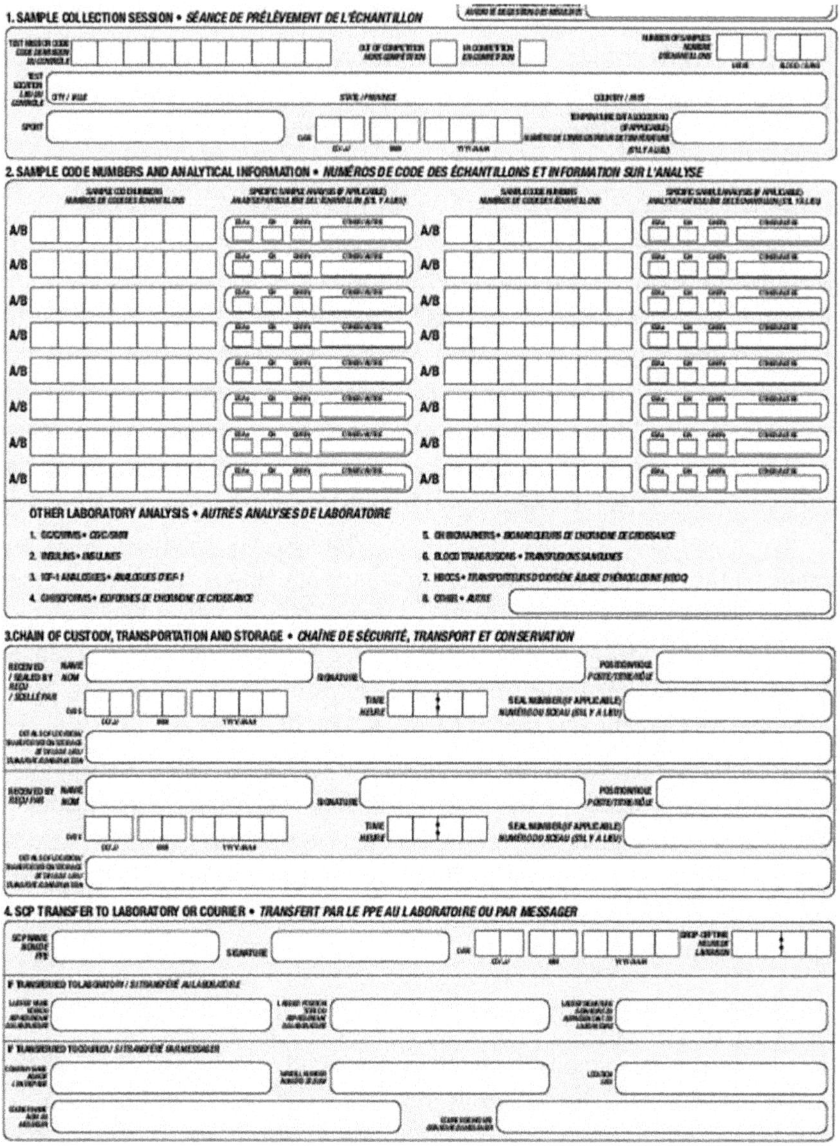

FIGURE 4.11 The chain of custody form. (https://www.wada-ama.org/sites/default/files/styles/resource_thumbnail_small/public/pdfpreview/038a227e1ef1789b611423268c79d051.jpg?itok=l3dFA4Wk.)

4.7 CONCLUSION

The step of data identification is an iterative process of identifying information sources regarding potentially relevant data. Data identification includes the use of accessible sources of information, part art and part research. Next, information classification identifies the complete set of data sources, who owns those data sources and what the data sources contain. From there, a researcher will discover precisely what information is available in each data source and decide which information needs to be obtained from each data source.

Big Data systems are massive, and gathering petabytes of data is rarely a viable option, so a researcher needs to be careful when deciding which information to collect. However, this caution must be tempered with the need for the first time to collect completely relevant data, as this data may not be available after the collection process has been completed.

BIBLIOGRAPHY

1. B. Davis, How much Data We Create Daily, 2013. http://goo.gl/a0lmFT.
2. P. Zikopoulos and C. Eaton, *Understanding Big Data: Analysis for Enterprise Class Hadoop and Streaming Data*. McGraw-Hill Osborne Media, New York, 2011.
3. B. Marr, Why Only One of the 5vs of Big Data Really Matters, 2015. http://goo.gl/azsnse.
4. E. Casey, *Digital Evidence and Computer Crime: Forensic Science, Computers, and the Internet*. Academic Press, Cambridge, MA, 2011.
5. S. Maukkamala and A.H. Sung, Identifying significant features for network forensic analysis using artificial intelligent techniques. *International Journal of Digital Evidences* 1.4, 1–17, 2003.
6. E. Casey, *Digital Evidences and Computer Crime*. Elsevier Inc., Amsterdam, 2011.
7. A. Guarino. Digital forensics as a big data challenges. In: H. Remier, N. Pohlmann, and W. Schneider (Eds.) *ISSE 2013 Securing Electronic Business Processes*. Springer Fachmedien Wiesbaden, Wiesbaden, 197–203, 2013.
8. T. Adams, *Introduction Forensics and Criminal Investigation*. Sage Publications, London, 2013.
9. J. Sremack, *Big Data Forensics: Learning Hadoop Investigations*. Packt Publishing, Birmingham, 2015.
10. L. Chaudhary and N. Shah, The Big Data a Growing Torrent of Technology, Compusoft, II (V), 2013.
11. J.W. Creswell, *Research Design: Qualitative, Quantitative, and Mixed Methods Aprroaches*. Sage, Omaha, NB, 2009.

12. B. Haram, Nigeria's Defence Budget Gulps $32.88bn, Says APC. Retrieved July 22, 2015 from thisdaylive.com, www.thisdaylive.com/articles/boko-haram-nigeria-s-defence-budgetgulps-32-88bn-says-apc/188650/EDRM.
13. EDRM, EDRM Stages. Retrieved June 19, 2015 from Electronic Discovery Reference Model, 2015. www.edrm.net/resources/edrm-stages-explained.
14. J. Joseph, *Why Computer Forensic Professionals shouldn't be Required to Have Private Investigator Licenses*. Science Direct. Elsevier, Nevada, 2014.
15. R. Kitchin, Big data, new epistemologies and paradigm shifts. *Big Data and Society* 1.1, 2014.
16. D. Lawton, eDiscovery in Digital Forensic Investigations. CAST Publication Number 32/14, 2014.
17. R.N. Levin, Pictorial Illustrations Still Improve Students Learning From Text, 2002.

CHAPTER 5

Security and Privacy in Big Data Access Controls

Ranjan Ganguli
All India Institute of Local Self Government-Deoghar

CONTENTS

5.1 INTRODUCTION

5.1.1 Big Data Is Not Big?

Big Data is a new area applied to many different data sets whose size cannot be expressed by commonly used software tools employed to timely manage, capture and analyze the vast volume of data.

Recent industry trends show that the growth rate of data gets doubled in every 2 years and will reach up to 40,000 exabytes in the coming year 2020 (IDC 2012). Big Data is not a technology, but a collection of various heterogeneous forms of data that arose from various sources, such as business transactions logs, systems logs, sensors, video and images, social media and medical transactions, and from almost all digital forms of data. Big Data has made a tremendous impact or gaining more attention after the advent of Internet of Things (IoT) where various forms of devices are connected on the Internet and produce a huge pool of data that needs to be transformed into meaning information. Additionally, public cloud service has made people more convenient through on-demand supply of hardware and software and generates intensive parallel data processing and high computing power. Thus, security and privacy issues are boosted through varieties and volumes (2Vs: volume and variety) of data to support Big Data-related applications.

As Big Data expands with the help of public clouds, traditional security solutions tailored to private computing infrastructures, confined to a well-defined security perimeter, such as firewalls and demilitarized zones (DMZs) are no more effective. Using Big Data, security functions are required to work over the heterogeneous composition of diverse hardware, operating systems and network domains. In this high-level computing environment, the important characteristics of software-defined networking (SDN) enable Big Data services on top of heterogeneous infrastructure. The abstraction form of SDN brings the separation of infrastructure being controlled and supervised from a higher control plane. Network administrator writes high-level control programs in contrast to conventional networks that separate network physical components like routers and switches, and codify functionally (through device manufacture) through low-level configuration of devices.

Using SDN, the intelligent management of secure functions can be implemented in a logically centralized controller, simplifying the following aspects: implementation of security rules, system (re)configuration and system evolution.

Using a hierarchy of controllers or through the usage of redundant controllers, the drawbacks of a centralized SDN solution can be less severe.

For safer communications and computing, the National Institute of Standard and Technology (NIST) launched a set of regulations and guidelines for different organizations. This is achieved through a systematic verification of system infrastructure in terms of risk assessment, responsiveness, recovery from attacks and protection against threats. Following the last verification principles, Defense Advanced Research Projects Agency (DARPA) is creating a program called Mining and Understanding Software Enclaves (MUSE) to enhance the quality of the US military's software. This program is designed to produce more robust software that can work with big data sets without causing errors or crashing under the sheer volume of information (DARPA 2014). In addition, security and privacy are becoming very urgent Big Data aspects that need to be tackled (Agrawal, Das, & El Abbadi 2011). To illustrate this, the social networks have enabled people to share and distribute valuable copyright-protected digital contents in a very easy way. Consequently, the copyright infringement behaviors, such as illicit copying, malicious distribution, unauthorized access and usage, and free sharing of copyright-protected digital contents, will become a much more common phenomenon. Thus, to make it less serious, Big Data must have solid solutions to support author's privacy and author's copyrights (Marques & Serrão 2013a). Also, users share more and more personal data and user-generated content (UGC) through their mobile devices and computers to social networks and cloud services, losing data and content control with a serious impact on their own privacy. Finally, one potentially promising approach is to create additional uncertainty for attackers by dynamically changing system properties in what is called a cyber moving target (MT) (Okhravi, Hobson, Bigelow, & Streilein 2014).

They present a summary of several types of MT techniques, consider the advantages and weaknesses of each and make recommendations for future research in this area.

5.2 BIG DATA CHALLENGES TO INFORMATION SECURITY AND PRIVACY

With the increase in a number of connections of devices in various networks and each other, the volume of data collected, stored and processed brings new challenges to information security every day. The present security mechanisms such as firewalls and DMZs are not sufficient for Big Data environment and extend out of the current organizations' network to fulfill data mobility and policies like bring your own device (BYOD). So, by considering the scenarios, the relevant question is, "What are adequate new policies and technologies available for Big Data that deal with privacy and security demands?" (Cloud Security Alliance 2013). The whole thing can be organized into four Big Data categories: infrastructure security, data management, data privacy and reactive security (e.g., monitoring attacks and anomalies).

In Big Data, a set of risk areas need to be addressed, such as information life cycle (classification of data, ownership and provenance), collection process, data creation and lack in security procedures. The security objectives of Big Data are no different from other types, that is, to preserve its availability, integrity and confidentiality.

Since Big Data is a complex and important topic nowadays, naturally the security and privacy challenges will arise (Michael & Miller 2013, Tankard 2012) on the 6Vs of Big Data that affect information security: variety, volume, velocity, value, variability and veracity (Figure 5.1). These have a direct impact on design, implementation and security solutions that are required to handle all these characteristics (Demchenko, Ngo, Laat, Membrey & Gordijenko 2014), but unfortunately, no such solutions exist as out of the box.

Cloud Security Alliance (CSA) is a nonprofit organization that has created a Big Data working group within a cloud computing environment for providing high-end security assurance focusing on the major challenges to implementing Big Data services (Cloud Security Alliance 2013). CSA has categorized the security and privacy challenges into four different aspects of the Big Data ecosystem: infrastructure security, data privacy, data integrity and management, and reactive security. According to CSA, these aspects face the following challenges:

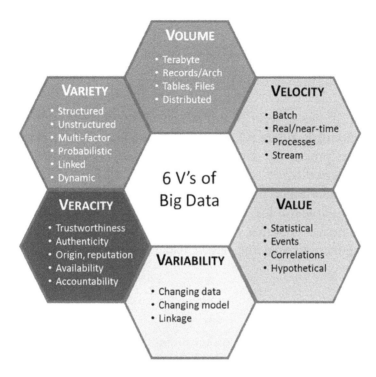

FIGURE 5.1 The six V's of Big Data. (Adapted from "IBM big data platform – Bringing big data to the Enterprise" 2014.)

- Infrastructure security
  1. Securing distributed processing of data,
  2. Best actions security for non-relational databases.
- Data privacy
  1. Contains data analysis using data mining preserving data privacy,
  2. Data security solutions using cryptography,
  3. Granular access control.
- Data integrity and management
  1. Storage and transaction logs security,
  2. Granular audits,
  3. Data origin.

- Reactive security

    1. End-to-end filtering and validation,

    2. Real-time security-level supervising.

These challenges of security and privacy of Big Data life cycle cover the entire spectrum. Figure 5.2 shows data in production (IoT devices), data itself, data processing, data storage, data transport and data usage on different devices.

A particular aspect of Big Data security and privacy has to be related to the rise of the IoT. IoT, defined by Oxford as "a proposed development of the Internet in which everyday objects have network connectivity, allowing them to send and receive data", is already a reality – Gartner

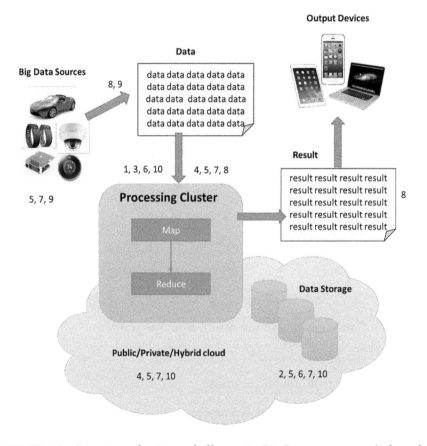

FIGURE 5.2 Security and privacy challenges in Big Data ecosystem. (Adapted from Cloud Security Alliance 2013.)

estimates that 26 billion of IoT devices will be installed by 2020, generating an incremental revenue of $300 billion (Rivera & van der Meulen 2014). The immense increase in the number of connected devices (cars, lighting systems, refrigerators, telephones, glasses, traffic control systems, health-monitoring devices, Supervisory Control and Data Acquisition (SCADA) systems, TVs, home security systems, home automation systems and many more) has led to manufacturers to push to the market, in a short period of time, a large set of devices, cloud systems and mobile applications to exploit this opportunity. While it presents tremendous benefits and opportunities for end-users, it is also responsible for security challenges.

A recent study conducted by HP on market-available IoT solutions products shows that 70% of those contain security problems. These problems are due to insufficient authorization, privacy issues, insecure web interface, lack of transport encryption and software protection (HP 2014). To consider the aforementioned findings, HP has started a project OWASP (Open Web Application Security Project) entitled as OWASP Internet of Things Top Ten (OWASP 2014). The main objective of this project is to help IoT suppliers to identify the top ten IoT security device problems and how to get rid of it. The OWASP project identify the following security concerns:

- **Insecure web interface:** It can allow an attacker to exploit an administration web interface (through cross-site scripting, cross-site request forgery and SQL injection) and to obtain unauthorized access to control the IoT device.

- **Insufficient authentication/authorization:** It can allow an attacker to exploit a bad password policy, break weak passwords and make access to privileged modes on the IoT device.

- **Insecure network services:** It can lead to an attacker exploiting unnecessary or weak services running on the device, or use those services as a jumping point to attack other devices on the IoT network.

- **Lack of transport encryption:** It can allow an attacker to eavesdrop data in transit between IoT devices and support systems.

- **Privacy concerns:** These concerns are raised from the fact the most IoT devices and support systems collect personal data from users and fail to protect that data.

- **Insecure cloud interface:** Without proper security controls, an attacker can use multiple attack vectors (insufficient authentication, lack of transport encryption, account enumeration) to access data or controls via the cloud website.

- **Insecure mobile interface:** Without proper security controls, an attacker can use multiple attack vectors (insufficient authentication, lack of transport encryption, account enumeration) to access data or controls via the mobile interface.

- **Insufficient security configurability:** Due to the lack or poor configuration mechanisms, an attacker can access data or controls on the device.

- **Insecure software/firmware:** Attackers can take advantage of unencrypted and unauthenticated connections to hijack IoT devices updates, and perform a malicious update that can compromise the device, a network of devices and the data they hold.

- **Poor physical security:** If the IoT device is physically accessible, then an attacker can use USB ports, SD cards or other storage means to access the device OS and potentially any data stored on the device.

It is clear that Big Data presents interesting opportunities for users and businesses; however, these opportunities are countered by enormous challenges in terms of privacy and security (Cloud Security Alliance 2013). Traditional security mechanisms are insufficient to provide a capable answer to those challenges. In the next section, some of these solutions/ proposals are going to be addressed.

5.3 ADDRESSING BIG DATA SECURITY AND PRIVACY CHALLENGES: A PROPOSAL

There is no single magical solution to solve the identified Big Data security and privacy challenges and traditional security solutions, which are mainly dedicated to protecting small amounts of static data, and are not adequate to the novel requisites imposed by Big Data services (Cloud Security Alliance 2013). There is a need to understand how the collection of large amounts of complex structured and unstructured data can be protected. Unauthorized access to that data to create new relations, combine different data sources and make it available to malicious users is a serious risk for Big Data. The basic and more common solution for this includes encrypting everything to make data secure regardless of where the data resides (data center, computer, mobile device or any other). As Big Data grows and its processing gets faster, encryption, masking and tokenization are critical elements for protecting sensitive data.

Due to its characteristics, Big Data projects need to take a holistic vision at security (Tankard 2012). Big Data projects need to take into consideration the identification of the different data sources, the origin and creators of data, as well as who is allowed to access the data. It is also necessary to make a correct classification to identify critical data, and align with the organization information security policy in terms of enforcing access control and data handling policies. As a recommendation, different security mechanisms should be closer to the data sources and data itself, in order to provide security right at the origin of data, and mechanisms of control and prevention on archiving, data leakage prevention and access control should work together (Kindervag, Balaouras, Hill, & Mak 2012).

The new Big Data security solutions should extend the secure perimeter from the enterprise to the public cloud (Juels & Oprea 2013). In this way, a trustful data provenance mechanism should also be created across domains. In addition, similar mechanisms to the ones used in Luo, Lin, Zhang and Zukerman (2013) can be used to mitigate distributed denial-of-service (DDoS) attacks launched against Big Data infrastructures. Also, security and privacy of Big Data are necessary to ensure data trustworthiness throughout the entire data life cycle – from data collection to usage.

The personalization feature of some Big Data services and its impact on the user privacy is discussed in Hasan, Habegger, Brunie, Bennani and Damiani (2013), who discuss these issues in the backdrop of EEXCESS, a concrete project aimed to both provide high-level recommendations and respect user privacy. A recent work describes proposed privacy extensions to UML to help software engineers to quickly visualize privacy requirements, and design them into Big Data applications (Jutla, Bodorik, & Ali 2013).

While trying to take the most of Big Data, in terms of security and privacy, it becomes mandatory that mechanisms that address legal requirements about data handling need to be met. Secure encryption technology must be employed to protect all the confidential data (Personally Identifiable Information (PII), Protected Health Information (PHI) and Intellectual Property (IP)), and careful cryptographic material (keys) access management policies need to be put in place, to ensure the correct locking and unlocking of data – this is particularly important for data stored. In order to be successful, these mechanisms need to be transparent to the end-user and have a low impact on the performance and scalability of data (software- and hardware-based encryptions mechanisms are to be considered) (Advantech 2013).

As previously referred, traditional encryption and anonymization of data are not adequate to solve Big Data problems. They are adequate to protect static information, but are not adequate when data computation is involved (MIT 2014). Therefore, other techniques, allowing specific and targeted data computation while keeping the data secret, need to be used. Secure Function Evaluation (SFE) (Lindell & Pinkas 2002), Fully Homomorphic Encryption (FHE) (Gentry 2009) and Functional Encryption (FE) (Goldwasser et al. 2014), and partition of data on noncommunicating data centers, can help in solving the limitations of traditional security techniques.

Homomorphic encryption is a form of encryption that allows specific types of computations (e.g., RSA public key encryption algorithm) to be carried out on ciphertext and generate an encrypted result, which, when decrypted, matches the result of operations performed on the plaintext (Gentry 2010). Fully homomorphic encryption has numerous applications, as referred in Van Dijk, Gentry, Halevi, and Vaikuntanathan (2010). This allows encrypted queries on databases, which keeps secret private user information where that data is normally stored (somewhere in the cloud – in the limit, a user can store its data on any untrusted server, but in encrypted form, without being worried about the data secrecy) (Ra Popa & Redfield 2011). It also enables private queries to a search engine – the user submits an encrypted query, and the search engine computes a succinct encrypted answer without ever looking at the query in the clear which could contain private user information such as the number of the national healthcare service. The homomorphic encryption also enables searching on encrypted data – a user stores encrypted files on a remote file server and can later have the server retrieve only files that (when decrypted) satisfy some Boolean constraint, even though the server cannot decrypt the files on its own. More broadly, the fully homomorphism encryption improves the efficiency of secure multiparty computation.

An important security and privacy challenge for Big Data is related to the storage and processing of encrypted data. Running queries against an encrypted database is a basic security requirement for secure Big Data; however, it is a challenging one. This raises the following questions: (i) Is the database encrypted with a single or multiple keys? (ii) Does the database need to be decrypted prior to running the query? (iii) Do the queries need to be also encrypted? (iv) Who has the permissions to decrypt the database? and many more. Recently, a system that was developed at MIT provides answers to some of these questions. CryptDB allows researchers to run database queries over encrypted data (Popa & Redfield 2011). Trustworthy applications that intent to query encrypted data will pass those queries to a CryptDB proxy (that sits between the application and the database) that rewrites those queries in a specific way so that they can be run against the encrypted database. The database returns the encrypted results back to the proxy, which holds a master key and will decrypt the results, sending the final answer back to the application. CryptDB supports numerous forms of encryption schemes that allow different types of operations on the data (Popa & Redfield 2012).

Apart from more specific security recommendations, it is also important to consider the security of the IT infrastructure itself. One of the common security practices is to place security controls at the edge of the networks; however, if an attacker violates this security perimeter, it will have access to all the data within it. Therefore, a new approach is necessary to move those security controls near to the data (or add additional ones). Monitoring, analyzing and learning from data usage and access is also an important aspect to continuously improve the security of the data-holding infrastructure and leverage the already-existing security solutions (Kindervag, Wang, Balaouras & Coit 2011, Kindervag et al. 2012).

5.4 DATA INTEGRITY IS NOT DATA SECURITY!

5.4.1 What Vs Why?

Consider an example of a pharmaceutical company; expecting a new drug to launch into the market but inspecting a team of higher production authority found that some quality aspects of control data are still missing. Such kinds of real-time compromised data integrity are common in many situations. Thus, accuracy and consistency of data are the major concerns found in many places of industries from minor to major significant business problems.

In this information age of Big Data where a huge volume of data is stored and processed, preserving data integrity is extremely important and a prime concern nowadays. To keep data safe, understanding the basics of data integrity and how it works is to be known in advance.

Data integrity means completeness, accuracy and consistency of data for a longer period of operation or no alteration between two frequent updates of data during a life cycle. Thus, compromised data is of little use in business enterprises as there is a chance of sensitive data loss. This enforces to create a core of data integrity in many enterprise security solutions. This is implemented through rules and standards, and collection of processes in the design phase. If the data integrity is secure, the overall information in a database will remain intact, reliable and accurate, no matter how long it is stored and often accessed. Data integrity also measures the degree of how data is safe from the outside world.

Solving compromised data is an essential part of enterprise security protocols. Data integrity is compromised in a various ways, which are as follows:

- **Human error:** When unintentional and malicious data is entered by the user.

- **Transfer (sending) error:** Data compromise or error occurs due to transfer data from one computer to others.

- Software bugs and viruses and other cyber threats.

- Hardware failure like device or hard disk crashes.

- Natural calamity, including fires and floods.

Some of the aforementioned compromises may be prevented through data security but data backup and duplication become a critical issue for ensuring integrity. Other best practices included in data integrity are input validation to check invalid entry; error detection to check data transmission errors; and security measures such as access control, data encryption and data loss prevention.

5.4.2 Data Integrity: Process Vs State

Considering data integrity either as a state or as a process creates confusion for many people. State defines data set as both valid and accurate, whereas process describes measures of accuracy and validity of data set or data in a database. Error checking and validation methods may be a part of the integrity process.

5.4.3 Integrity Types

For both hierarchical and relational databases, there are two types of data integrity: physical integrity and logical integrity (including entity, domain, referential and user-defined entities), which are a collection of processes and methods that enforce data integrity in both of the databases.

5.4.3.1 Physical Integrity

Physical integrity deals with the protection of wholeness and accuracy of data in storing and fetching process. This integrity is compromised when disasters like hackers disrupt database functions or power goes out. Storage erosion, human error and other issues also make it impossible for application programmers, managers, system programmers and internal auditors to find accurate data.

5.4.3.2 Logical Integrity

This integrity is concerned with rationality or correctness of data and keeps data unchanged when it is used in a relational database. It protects data from intruders and hackers but in different ways than physical integrity. Methods to ensure logical integrity are foreign key constraint, checksum, run-time check and program assertions. There are four types of logical integrity, which are as follows:

5.4.3.3 Entity Integrity

This integrity ensures that columns in the database have unique and non-null values. Primary key ensures the integrity in a relational database. For example, employee number can be considered as a primary key of employee database and should not contain a null value and can be linked and used in other ways.

5.4.3.4 Referential Integrity

Referential Integrity (RI) is a property stating that data being referenced are valid in a relational table. Foreign keys are a second table which can be referred to as primary key (generally a primary or parent table) in the first table. It measures the consistency and accuracy of data between relationships.

5.4.3.5 Domain Integrity

This integrity ensures the accuracy of a piece of data entered in the column of a database. It is defined by various data types such as integer, character or decimal. In general, the idea is that every value in a column has a finite set of possible values: Column defined as "INT NOT NULL" can only have a valid 32-bit integer in it, whereas column defined as "CHAR (1) NULL" can be NULL or any valid, single character. It also refers to common ways to input and read data: If a database uses transaction values to include dollars and cents, then three decimals will not be allowed.

5.4.3.6 User-Defined Integrity

Sometimes RI and domain integrity are not enough to protect data. User-defined or business integrity ensures that database includes business rules, policies, regulations and various procedures. Business integrity is enforced by triggers and stored procedures. This integrity is created by users to meet their particular needs.

5.5 INFILTRATION ACTIVITIES: FRAUD DETECTION WITH PREDICTIVE ANALYTICS

The growing rate of Big Data has affected malware analysis also. Today, increased computational power and storage capacities for Big Data processing system have the ability to handle an increased volume of data being collected and execute new ways of analyzing and visualizing malware developed.

5.6 CASE STUDY I: IN A SECURE SOCIAL APPLICATION

Millions of people are connected on a daily basis to a social network. Thus, social network is the fastest way to communicate with other and becomes attractive in nature nowadays and has the ability to expose own network of friends to others, creating a bridge of relationship between user and content (McKenzie et al. 2012). By taking advantage of this functionality, people share various kinds of digital content with others, which may be their direct contacts or indirect (i.e., other one's connections). This medium of sharing is extremely powerful for the next-level social interaction. But, on the other hand, it raises a serious concern of privacy and security because sharing control is not on the end-user side. This may create a serious threat to user privacy as most of their contents are shared and easily available to a wider audience in just a few seconds. For general people, it is very hard to control specific sharing properties of the contents placed in the network and stayed under control.

Emergence of Web 2.0 has changed simply users from information consumers to important content producers. This User Generated Content (UGC) is developed voluntarily by any individual or consortium and shared across on an online platform. This user-generated extensive volume of data is available through several platforms and grows continuously in size (Kim, Jin, Kim, & Shin 2012).

Currently, social networks presented a predefined set of contents related to privacy and security sharing controls (Chen & Shi 2009). Major social network sites offer users to share their contents under specific privacy rules, which are defined by social platform, not by the end-user. These rules vary from platform to platform and are extremely permissive. Sometimes, contents are shared in a non-protected manner and become easy for unauthorized usage and sharing by others. Subsequent privacy policy changes are being made that threaten more and more the user to protect their personal information and personal content.

Most of the times the problems linked with the security and privacy of content shared on the social network are related to the security of social network platform used itself. The exploitation of such a platform may lead to security and privacy threats. Sometimes allegations may arise about the cooperation of some of the most renowned IT suppliers with government agencies to allow the unauthorized access to user's information and content. In theory, this fact is quite relevant as a social network service provider has the permission to access unlimited information and content of all its users.

This are an increased number of problems in contrast to both end-user and organizations. More and more organizations, institutions and others rely on social network platform to spread information, create relations with employees and customers, involve in knowledge capture and dissemination. These new ways of communication and interaction are very pertinent topics for both end-users and organizations in respect of both privacy and security.

The continuous growth of connecting mobile devices (mostly smartphones, tablets and IoTs) with capabilities to produce multimedia-related contents such as audio, video and text or pictures is at the palm of every user's hand; following them everywhere and anytime accessible is also a serious threat to their privacy and security (De Cristofaro, Soriente,

Tsudik, & Williams 2012). Also, this content creates cultural, symbolic and affective benefits, including personal satisfaction, civic engagement or community building and improved functionality for devices. In other words, this checks whether user contents create value and economic development or not.

Taking all these into consideration, it is clear that there must be a separation between social network platform providers, their functionalities and the content that they hold. A transparent mechanism needs to create to transfer a part of the security and privacy content to the end-user. In this segment, it is proposed a paradigm shift from the current social networks' security and privacy scenario to another paradigm that empowers social network users on the control and safeguard of its privacy, passing user-generated control to end-user through proper right management system (Marques & Serrão 2013b). Also, the storage and protection entity is independent of the social network platform used. This approach will create a mechanism that safeguards the shared UGC on the social network platform and provides access control to the end-user.

5.6.1 Overall System Architecture

As referred to previous section, the approach followed is open rights management system based on Open **Secure Digital Rights Management** (SDRM) **Solution** (Serrão 2008, Serrão, Neves, Barker, & Balestri 2003). Open SDRM is an open and distributed rights management architecture that allows other business models to implement. It is created taking into consideration interoperability aspects (Serrão, Rodriguez, & Delgado 2011) that allow other modules to be reintegrated and decoupled to allow interoperability with other non-Open SDRM using open and well-defined Application Programming Interface (API) (Figure 5.3). Also, there may exist more than one instance of each of the services on the platform, allowing scalability and growth of all possible configuration options (Serrão, Dias, & Delgado 2005).

For the proposed system, rights management system can be integrated with the social network platform. Like UNIX, if social network uses it as an open-source development of API, a tighter scenario can be achieved. Otherwise, the use of other publicly available mechanisms on the platform enables a lesser-integrated scenario and violates privacy and security concerns. Using mechanism on the platform is the most common situation, and the approach will be reflected here.

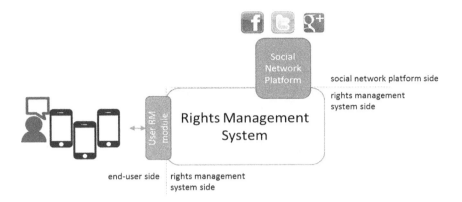

FIGURE 5.3   Overview of the architecture integrated with the rights management system.

Some elements of this architecture cooperate in order to provide functionalities to both the end-user and the social platform network in order to implement the necessary security and privacy mechanisms to end-user-generated content.

Open SDRM is composed of different services, as shown in Figure 5.4. The whole services are working as server and end-user model. Some services are deployed in the server side, while other services are implemented in the user side wherein the authorization service handles the requests to render some types of content on the user device, processes requests and

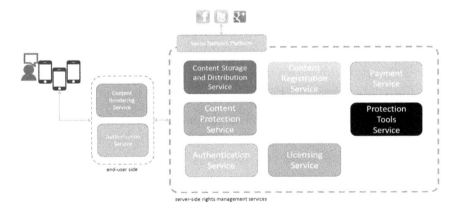

FIGURE 5.4   Overview of the architecture integrated with the rights management system with different services.

matches with existing credentials, permissions authority and license to provide the content. The end-user side service is responsible for verifying the necessary requirements to render the content and effectively provide the contents for the end-user.

The server side handles the large part of rights management system. A set of components with well-defined API allows integration to implement the specific business model. Following are the services:

- **Content storage and distribution service:** This service is mainly for storage and distribution of user content in a protected content.

- **Content Protection Service (CPS):** This service is mainly for the protection of the content. The content is protected by specific protection tools and mechanisms that may change per the business model that is going to be implemented.

- **Content Registration Service (CRGS):** This service is mainly responsible for registering the content on the platform that will be used to identify the content of the system. This unique identifier is used for the entire life cycle to identify the UGC.

- **Payment service:** This service is responsible for communicating with a payment gateway if the business model includes trade content that implements the necessary mechanisms to process payments.

- **Protection Tools Service (PTS):** This service is responsible for registering content protection tools available on the system when implementing the content protection schemas.

- **Authentication Service (AS):** This service handles the registration of users on the system as well as the requests for authentic users on behalf of other services.

- **Licensing Service (LS):** This is one of the most important services of the rights management framework, mainly for creating license templates, producing new content licenses and providing licenses, upon request, to specific users.

This section of this document will provide a description on "how a general user can utilize this platform to share UGC on the social network and how a user can access content shared by other users".

5.6.2 Registration on the Platform

This platform already assumes that all the system services are initially registered on the platform either from the server side or from the client side. This registration process assigns unique credentials to each one of the services used for all kinds of future interactions and ensures that they are uniquely registered and differentiated from other services (Figure 5.5). This registration process is the central mechanism, is conducted by the AS and issues credentials to all the other services. Also, the communication is done between services over a secure and authenticated channel using Secure Sockets Layer/Transport Layer Security (SSL/TLS), ensuring authentication and security of the servers where the services are deployed and establish a secure communication channel (Thomas 2000).

1. The AS contains cryptographic material (KpubAS, KprivAS) with credentials like CASAS that are self-issued or issued by another entity (CCAAS).

2. Service that needs registration generates a key pair (KpubS, KprivS) and sends a registration request to AS with Sinfo and the public key (KpubS) of the service: Sinfo + KpubS.

3. After verifying information by AS, it creates a unique service identifier (SUUID) and service credentials that will identify this service globally and uniquely on the platform: CASS [UUID] = KprivAS {SUUID, KpubS [UUID], CASAS}. After signing the credentials by AS, it is returned to the requesting service.

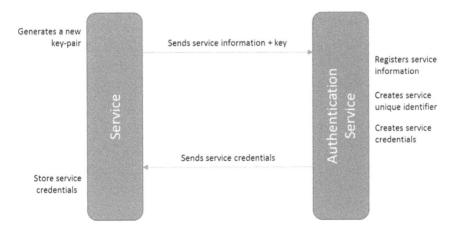

FIGURE 5.5 Handling the registration of new services on the platform.

4. The requesting service stores the credentials that contain the public key of the AS (KpubAS). It is used to prove credentials of other entities that also rely on the same AS, that trust the service of AS, that trust on the credentials issued by AS and that are presented by other services.

This registration process repeated several times based on the services available within a social platform. This enables a trusted ecosystem of services on the platform. Another important thing in the registration process is to register a user on the rights management system, which may be dependent or independent of the social network platform (Figure 5.6). The process is as follows:

1. Consider that the user has no account on the social network platform, and the user starts the registration process on the social network. To do that, the user needs to supply their email (as username) and password.

2. A confirmation message is sent to the end-user that the registration process is complete.

3. Next, the user using the client-side rights management Authorization Service (AUTS) initializes the registration process in the rights management platform by providing several options to end-user (integrated with social network platform and other modes). For this, the user will use different registration options by the mode of integrated authentication.

4. On the AUTS, the user introduces social account credentials (email, password) and starts the authentication process. On successful registration, the social network returns an access token that has a specific validity and a set of permission rules to conduct different operations on the social network in respect of the end-user.

1. By using the user credentials (email, password), AUTS creates a secret key that is used to initialize a secure storage on the authorization service: $S^{SStorage} = SHA1[email + password]$.

2. The AUTS securely stores the user information, and the social network returns an access token. Additionally, the AUTS creates a key pair for the (K_{pub}^U, K_{priv}^U).

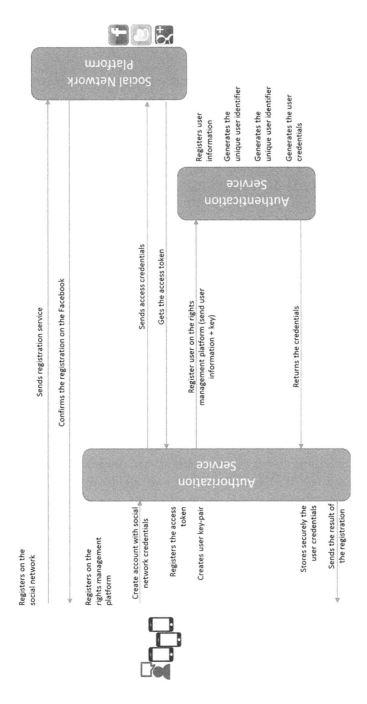

FIGURE 5.6   Overview of the user registration process.

3. AUTS contacts the AS to register the user on the platform. This is performed using the CASS[AUTS] that contains the K_{pub}^{AS}. CASS[AUTS] is also sent to ensure that the AUTS has been previously registered: K_{pub}^{AS} (email, $K_{pub,CASS[AUTS]}^{U}$).

4. The AUTS receives all this information. After deciphering it and validating the AUTS credential, it registers the user information, generates a unique identifier for the user and creates credentials for the user: $C_{UUID}^{AS} = K_{priv}^{AS} \{UUID, K_{pub}^{U}\}$.

5. The credentials are returned to the AUTS and are securely stored: $S_{k}^{\text{SStorage}}\left(C_{UUID}^{AS}\right)$. The user is notified about the result of the registration operation. This is the concluding step of the service and user registration on the rights management platform. The user is now prepared to use both the rights management service and social network platform.

5.6.3 Sharing Content on the Platform

Other important functionality on the social network is to share the UGC, and this mechanism is performed by using rights management platform and the content stored securely on a configured location (either on the social platform, on the specific storage location or on the rights management platform). When the user uploads UGC, the content is protected and the rights, permissions and restrictions about the content can be defined by the user.

It is considered that both the users (who has generated the content and who is willing to access the content) are properly registered and authenticated on the social network and rights management platform (Figure 5.7). Thus, in brief, the UGC is uploaded to the rights management platform, access rights and permission are user-defined, the content is protected, and a URI is returned to be shared on the social network platform.

Now, the mechanism of the sharing process described above is defined as follows:

1. The user sends the UGC to be shared on the social network and uploaded through the Content Rendering Service (CRS). This service needs user credentials (email, password), if not yet authenticated. These log-in credentials are used to access the secure storage: $Sk^{\text{SStorage}} = SHA1[\text{email} + \text{password}]$.

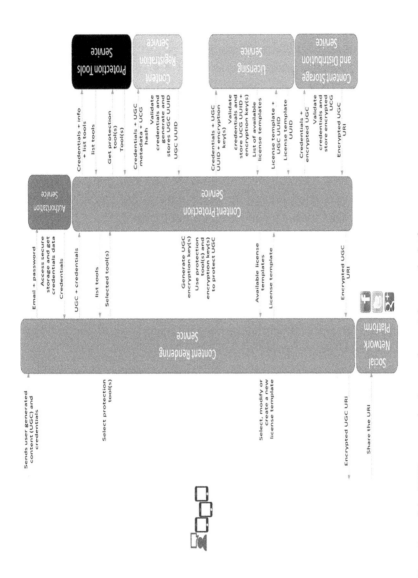

FIGURE 5.7   Overview of the UGC secure sharing on the social network platform.

2. AUTS reads from the secure storage, the user rights management system credentials: CASUUID with the help of CRS.

3. This CRS uploads to CPS; the UGC sends user credentials received in the previous step: UGCUUID, CASUUID.

4. After receiving some metadata information about UGC (such as type, format and encoding, among others) by CPS, the PTS provides a list of available protection tools that are suitable to protect the UGC. The PTS sends its credentials and some information about the content: CASCPS, UGC_info.

5. PTS returns a list of protection tools that match with the request made by CPS, and it is signed by PTS: KprivPTS{protection_tools_list}.

6. CPS returns a list of protection tools to CRS and presents it to the user. The user then selects the most appropriate one to adjust the parameters of tools to the UGC and submits their request about required protection tools.

7. CPS requests the selected protection from PTS, and the PTS returns to the CPS as per the requests.

8. CPS requests the CRGS for the UGC to be registered, and for this, the CPS sends its credentials along with metadata and content hash: CASCPS, UGC_info,SHA1[UGC].

9. The CRGS stores information and generates a unique content identifier that is returned to CPS: KprivCRS.{UGCUUID}.

10. One or more content encryption keys (CEK[1], CEK[2] … CEK[n]) are generated by CPS that is applied over the UGC, using the selected protection tools, in order to ensure the appropriate content protection.

11. Following this protection process, at the LS, the CPS sends the content encryption keys for registration. Each of the content encryption keys is protected with the user key, and the entire message is protected by the CPS key: CASCPS, KpubCPS (KpubU (CEK[1], CEK[2] … CEK[n]), UGCUUID).

12. After validating, LS receives information and returns a list of templates to the CPS. The CPS returns a list of licensing templates to CRS, and the user selects the most appropriate template and either creates it, modifies it or adopts it.

13. The CPS receives the licensing template (LIC_{TPL}) and sends it to LS, which associates with UGC identifier LIC_{TPL}, UGCUUID. At last, LS returns the license template identifier (LIC_{TPL} [UUID]).

14. In the next stage, CPS sends protected UGC to content storage and distribution service, which stores encrypted content: CASCPS, KprivCPS{CEK[n](UGC), UGCUUID}.

15. For the location of stored encrypted UGC, the content storage and distribution service returns URI, and in the next step, it will be shared on the social network platform.

On completion of the process, the UGC is shared on the social network platform and the user can use the social network-sharing mechanism to control the way of propagation of UGC on the social network. But, to get a good control over UGC, the user needs rights management system to produce specific licenses with the conditions under which the UGC can be used. These licenses have various formats (either in ODRL or in MPEG-21 REL) used to support the expression of rights over the UGC. Thus, on uploading UGCs to the rights management system and on executing the previous steps, the following are the subsequent steps:

1. To obtain the appropriate license template for the specific UGC created before, the CPS contacts LS: LIC_{TPL} [UUID]. This license template is an XML-formatted document that is associated with parameterized fields that can be adapted to specific rights situations.

2. A license template for UGC is made up of the following things:

    a. Unique identifiers of the users (UUID), multiple users (UUID1, UUID2,..., UUIDn) or a group identifier (GUUID).

    b. The unique identifier of content as UGCUUID.

    c. Permissions list (Permission1...Permissionn).

    d. Restrictions list (Restriction1...Restrictionn).

    e. Validity date (validity).

    f. Different encryption keys of content as (CEK[1], CEK[2] ... CEK[n]), and it is protected with user public key:: KpubU (CEK[1], CEK[2] ... CEK[n]).

    g. License signature where the license contents are signed by the LS:
License = KprivLIS {$UUID_1$ ... $UUID_n$, $GUUID_1$, $GUUID_n$, UGCUUID, $Permission_1$...$(Permission)_n$ $Restriction_1$... $(Restriction)_n$, Validity, KpubU (CEK[1]... CEK[n].

3. The license is stored on the LS, where it can be accessed by legitimate users.

5.6.4 Accessing Content on the Platform

The final process in the case study is how users can access others' UGC that is shared on the social network platform. To do so, the user needs to be registered on the social network platform and the rights management system. On navigating through the social network platform timeline, the shared UGC on the social network platform is presented in the form of URI, and when clicked, it is interpreted by the rights management platform and the access process started.

5.7 CASE STUDY II

5.7.1 An Intelligent Intrusion Detection/Prevention System on a Software-Defined Network

Consider a case study of an intelligent Intrusion Detection/Prevention System (IDS/IPS) in a software-defined network, and this IDS/IPS behavior is controlled by a Kinetic module (Feamster 2014). The Kinetic language (Monsanto, Reich, Foster, Rexford, & Walker 2013) is an SDN control framework where operators can define a network policy as a Finite State Machine (FSM). Dynamic events of different types in the network triggered between different FSMs (e.g., intrusion detection, host state). Depending on different network events, operators enforce different policies using the FSM model. Python language is used to implement Kinetic – a Pyretic controller module.

"A Kinetic control allows programmer-defined events to dynamically change forwarding behavior of a set of flows. Such kinds of events range from topology changes (generated by Pyretic runtime) to security incidents (generated by intrusion detection system). A set of description of FSM states are specified by the programmer, each of which maps to some network behavior is encoded using Pyretic's policy language; and a set of transitions between those states, each triggered by events defined by the operator" (Feamster 2014).

This case study implements an IDS/IPS security module, which includes the following:

- The host must be dropped if it is infected and not privileged.

- But if a host is infected somehow and is privileged, then the host must be automatically redirected to a garden wall host, where corrected security actions are carried out over that infected host (such as clean and install security patches to recover it).

- If the host is not infected, then the traffic from the host is forwarded toward its destination.

5.7.2 The Code Reveals

In Table 5.1, a partial view of the Kinetic control program using Python is used to evaluate the intelligent IDS/IPS. To become clearer, this code functionality is explained in the following paragraph.

Each time a new packet arrives at the system; the IDS/IPS initially processes that packet and defines the policy to be applied to that packet (i.e., drop|redirect|forward). This policy is then delivered to a second module that implements further MAC functionality, namely, the learning algorithm of MAC addresses to enhance the L2 packet forwarding. This is the module that effectively forwards or redirects the packet (otherwise if the packet is to be drooped, this second module will not receive any packet at all as it was rejected by the first IDS/IPS module).

The code shown in Table 5.1 corresponds to the IDS/IPS module, and its code is encapsulated inside a class designated by "gardenwall", which was instantiated from the class called "DynamicPolicy" (taking care of the processing of JSON events). The function "lpec" is like a packet input filter because it only selects the packets whose source IP address is specified by variable *srcip*. This function aims to process the first packet of a flow exactly in the same way as all the following packets of that flow. In this example, a transition function is used, which encodes logic shows that new value a state variable should take in response to an event arrives at the controller. Likewise, the infected transition function encodes a single case: When an *infected* event occurs, the state variable that is taken new value *infected* is the value of that event (i.e., FALSE or TRUE). This is an example of an exogenous transition (i.e., the state variable *infected* is changed by an external event); another exogenous transition in this scenario is the one associated with the

TABLE 5.1   Snapshot of the Code for the Module IDS/IPS

```
class gardenwall(DynamicPolicy):
    def _init_ (self):
        # Garden Wall
        def redirectToGardenWall():
            client_ips = [IP('10.0.0.1'), IP('10.0.0.2')]
            rewrite_policy = rewriteDstIPAndMAC(client_ips,
 '10.0.0.3') return rewrite_policy
        ### DEFINE THE LPEC FUNCTION
        def lpec(f):
            return match(srcip=f['srcip'])
        ## SET UP TRANSITION FUNCTIONS
        @transition
        def exempt(self):
            self.case(occurred(self.event),self.event)
        @transition
        def infected(self):
            self.case(occurred(self.event),self.event)
        @transition
        def policy(self):
            # If exempt, redirect pkt to gardenwall;rewrite
 dstip to 10.0.0.3
            self.case(test_and_true(V('exempt'),
 V('infected')),
 C(redirectToGardenWall()))
            # If infected, drop pkt
            self.case(is_true(V('infected')),C(drop))
            # Else, identity -> forward pkt
            self.default(C(identity))
        ### SET UP THE FSM DESCRIPTION
        self.fsm_def = FSMDef(
            infected=FSMVar(type=BoolType(),
                            init=False,
                            trans=infected),
            exempt=FSMVar(type=BoolType(),
                            init=False,
                            trans=exempt),
            policy=FSMVar(type=Type(Policy,
                    {drop,identity,redirectToGardenWall()}),
                            init=identity,
                            trans=policy))
        ### SET UP POLICY AND EVENT STREAMS
        fsm_pol = FSMPolicy(lpec,self.fsm_def)
        json_event = JSONEvent()
        json_event.register_callback(fsm_pol.event_handler)
        super(gardenwall,self). _init_ (fsm_pol)
```

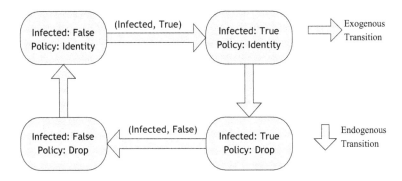

FIGURE 5.8   Finite State Machine (FSM) (Feamster 2014).

state variable *exempt*. In opposition, the transition associated with the state variable *policy* is endogenous because its state is triggered by both internal state variables of the current FSM: *infected* and *exempt*.

The FSM (see Figure 5.8) used in the current situation associates transition function defined previously with appropriate state variables. The FSM contains a set of state variables definition, and each variable definition specifies the variable's types (set of allowable values), initial value and corresponding transition functions. The infected is a Boolean variable whose initial value is FALSE (making assumptions that hosts are not infected), and the transition is based on the infected function defined previously. Likewise, drop or identity is taken by policy variables and initially starts in the identity state, and transitions are based on the policy function defined previously. FSM Policy that Kinetic provides automatically directs each incoming external event to the appropriate lpec FSM, where it will be handled by the exogenous transition function specified in the FSM description (i.e., the function self.fsm_def). This is the way it is ensured that FSM works as expected.

5.7.3 Evaluation

The network topology used in the current evaluation made with a network emulator is shown in Figure 5.9, and all of its evaluation was performed in a single Ubuntu Linux virtual machine.

We now initiate the evaluation, open a Linux shell and run our Kinetic controller application with the following commands:

```
$ cd ~/pyretic

$ pyretic.py pyretic.kinetic.examples.gardenwall
```

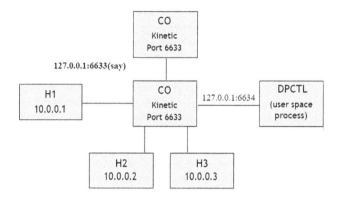

FIGURE 5.9   Test of network topology (Feamster 2014).

As shown in Figure 5.10, the Kinetic controller prints out results after the verification of network policies using NuSMV symbolic model checker (NuSMV 2014). Kinetic automatically generates a NuSMV input from the program written by the programmer or operator and verifies logic statements written in CTL (Computation Tree Logic) (CTL 2014).

In a second shell, we start the network emulator "mininet", performing the following command:

```
$ sudo mn --controller=remote --topo=single,3--mac
  -arp
```

The visualized output result is shown in Figure 5.11. In addition, the bottom line of Figure 5.12 shows that the emulated switch is discovered by the Kinetic controller.

Imagine a situation now that host "h1" becomes compromised (infected). This situation originates from the transmission of an event to change the state of the FSM in a way that any traffic originated in that host should be discarded in the switch. In this network status, the traffic ICMP between hosts "h1" and "h2" becomes blocked. We issue the transmission of the "infected" event to the controller executing in a third terminal the following command:

```
$ python json _ sender.py -n infected -l True
  --flow="{srcip=10.0.0.1}" -a

127.0.0.1-p 50001
```

The "infected" event was sent to the controller as it is possible to be visualized in Figure 5.13.

```
*** Please report bugs to <numsv-users@fbk.eu>

*** Copyright (c) 2010, Fondazione Bruno Kessler

*** This version of NuMSV is linked to the CUDD library version 2.4.1

*** Copyright (c) 1995-2004, Regents of the University of Colorado

*** This version of NuMSV is linked to the MiniSat SAT solver.

*** See http://www.cs.chalmers.se/Cs/Research/FormalMethods/MiniSat

*** Copyright (c) 2003-2005, Niklas Een, Niklas Sorensson


-- specification AG ((infected & !exempt) -> AX policy = policy_1) is true

-- specification AG (!infected -> AX policy = policy_2) is true

-- specification AG ((infected & exempt) -> AX policy = policy_3) is true

-- specification A [ policy = policy_2 U infected ] is true system diameter: 3

reachable states: 12 (2^3.58496) out of 12 (2^3.58496)

======================= NuSMV Output End =====================


POX 0.1.0 (betta) / Copyright 2011-2013 James McCauley, et al. Connected to
pyretic frontend.

INFO:core:POX 0.1.0 (betta) is up.
```

FIGURE 5.10 Kinetic controller terminal.

```
mininet@mininet-vm:~$ sudo mn --controller=remote --topo=single, 3 --mac --arp
*** Creating network
*** Adding controller
*** Adding hosts:
h1 h2 h3
*** Adding switches:
s1
*** Adding links:
(h1, s1) (h2, s1) (h3, s1)
*** Configuring hosts
h1 h2 h3
*** Startting controller
*** Startting 1 switches
s1
*** Startting CLI:
mininet>
```

FIGURE 5.11 Mininet terminal.

```
*** Copyright (c) 2010, Fondazione Bruno Kessler
*** This version of NuMSV is linked to the CUDD library version 2.4.1
*** Copyright (c) 1995-2004, Regents of the University of Colorado
*** This version of NuMSV is linked to the MiniSat SAT solver.
*** See http://www.cs.chalmers.se/Cs/Research/FormalMethods/MiniSat
*** Copyright (c) 2003-2005, Niklas Een, Niklas Sorensson

-- specification AG ((infected & !exempt) -> AX policy = policy_1) is true
-- specification AG (!infected -> AX policy = policy_2) is true
-- specification AG ((infected & exempt) -> AX policy = policy_3)   is true
-- specification A [ policy = policy_2  U infected ]   is true
system diameter: 3
reachable states: 12 (2^3.58496) out of 12 (2^3.58496)
===================== NuSMV Output End =====================

POX 0.1.0 (betta) / Copyright 2011-2013 James McCauley, et al.
Connected to pyretic frontend.
INFO:core:POX 0.1.0 (betta) is up.
INFO: openflow.of_01: [None 1] closed
INFO: openflow.of_01: [00-00-00-00-00-01 2] connected
```

FIGURE 5.12   Switch contacts the controller.

```
mininet@mininet-vm:~/pyretic/pyretic/kinetic$ python json_sender.py -n infected -l
True --flow ="{srcip=10.0.0.1}" -a 127.0.0.1 -p 50001

Flow_Str = {srcip=10.0.0.1}

Data Payload = {'dstip': None, 'protocol': None, 'srcmac': None, 'tos': None,
'vlan_pcp': None, 'dstmac': None, 'inport': None, 'switch': None, 'ethtype': None,
'srcip': '10.0.0.1', 'dstport': None, 'srcport': None, 'vlan_id': None}

Ok
mininet@mininet-vm:~/pyretic/pyretic/kinetic$
```

FIGURE 5.13   JSON event transmitted.

After milliseconds of executions, the Kinetic controller received the event informing that host h1 is infected (see Figure 5.14). As a result of this, the controller changed the policy to drop the packets originated by host "h1".

After this, we have tried to send two ping messages from host "h1" to host "h2" as is shown in Figure 5.15 without any success. This occurs because the IDS/IPS is installed in the switch between "h1" and "h2" using a policy to drop the packets originated by host "h1".

Next, assuming that host "h1" was classified as a privileged (exempt) terminal, the controller will be notified from this through the following event:

```
-- specification A [ policy = policy_2 U infected]     is true

system diameter: 3

reachable states: 12 (2^3.58496) out of 12 (2^3.58496)

======================= NuSMV Output End =====================

POX 0.1.0 (betta) / Copyright 2011-2013 James McCauley, et al.
Connected to pyretic frontend.

INFO:core:POX 0.1.0 (betta) is up. INFO:
openflow.of_01: [None 1] closed

INFO: openflow.of_01: [00-00-00-00-00-01 2] connected

Received connection from ('127.0.0.1', 42143)

Received event infected is True related with flow {'srcip':10.0.0.1}
fsm_policy:event_name = infected

fsm_policy:event_value = True

fsm_policy:event_state= {'policy':drop, 'infected':True, 'exempt':False}
fsm_policy:self.policy = if
    match: ('srcip', 10.0.0.1) then
    [DynamicPolicy] drop
else
    identity
```

FIGURE 5.14   Controller changes the policy to drop packets.

```
s1
*** Adding links:

(h1, s1) (h2, s1)(h3,s1)

*** Configuring hosts
h1 h2 h3

*** Startting controller

*** Startting 1 switches
s1
*** Startting CLI:
mininet> h1 ping -c 2 h2

PING 10.0.0.2 (10.0.0.2) 56(84) bytes of data.

--- 10.0.0.2 ping statistics     ---

2 packets transmitted, 0 received, 100% packet loss, time 1008ms
mininet>
```

FIGURE 5.15   ICMP traffic is dropped.

```
$ python json_sender.py -n exempt -l True
--flow="{srcip=10.0.0.1}" -a

127.0.0.1-p 50001
```

Immediately after, Kinetic controller received the event informing that host "h1" is infected (see Figure 5.16). As a consequence of this, the controller changed the policy to redirect the packets originated by host "h1" to host "h3" (policy modify) for further analysis. This policy is installed in the switch.

After we repeat the ping command, there is a redirection of traffic from host "h1", which is perfectly visible in Figure 5.17. One can note that the host replying to the ping is host "h3" instead of "h2". As explained earlier, host "h3" is responsible to recover, in terms of security, any privileged hosts that by some reason become compromised.

After some corrective actions are performed in host "h1" by "h3", one can assume that host "h1" has recovered. In this way, a new event is sent to the controller notifying that host "h1" is changed to the state of "not infected", as follows:

```
fsm_policy:event_name=
infected fsm_policy:event_value=
True

fsm_policy:event_state= {'policy': drop, 'infected': True, 'exempt': False}
fsm_policy:self.policy = if

  match: ('srcip', 10.0.0.1)
then

  [DynamicPolicy]
  drop

else

  identity

Received connection from ('127.0.0.1', 42144)

Received event exempt is True related with flow {'srcip': 10.0.0.1}
fsm_policy:event_name= exempt

fsm_policy:event_value= True

fsm_policy:event_state= {'policy': modify: ('dstip', 10.0.0.3)
('dstmac', 00:00:00:00:00:03), 'infected':True,

'exempt': True} fsm_policy:self.policy = if

  match: ('srcip', 10.0.0.1)
then
  [DynamicPolicy]
  modify: ('dstip', 10.0.0.3) ('dstmac', 00:00:00:00:00:03)
else
  identity
```

FIGURE 5.16   Changed policy to redirect the traffic.

```
mininet> h1 ping -c 2 h2
PING 10.0.0.2 (10.0.0.2) 56(84) bytes of data.
64 bytes from 10.0.0.3 icmp_req=1 ttl=64 time=115 ms
64 bytes from 10.0.0.3 icmp_req=2 ttl=64 time=112 ms

--- 10.0.0.2 ping statistics ---
2 packets transmitted, 2 received, 0% packet loss, time 1002ms
rtt min/avg/mdev = 112.492/114.106/115.720/1.614 ms
mininet>
```

FIGURE 5.17   ICMP traffic is redirected.

```
match: ('switch', 1) ('dstmac', 00:00:00:00:00:01)
then
   [DynamicPolicy]
   fwd 1
else
   flood on:
   -------------------------------------------------------------------------
   switch  |  switch edges  |  egress ports                                |
   -------------------------------------------------------------------------
   1       |                | 1[2]---, 1[3]---, 1[1]---                     |
Received connection from ('127.0.0.1', 42145)
Received event infect is False related with flow {'srcip': 10.0.0.1}
fsm_policy:event_name= infected
fsm_policy:event_value= False
fsm_policy:event_state= {'policy': identity, 'infected': False, 'exempt': True}
fsm_policy:self.policy = if
   match: ('srcip', 10.0.0.1)
then
   [DynamicPolicy]
   identity
else
   identity
```

FIGURE 5.18   Policy back to traffic pass through identity.

```
$ python json_sender.py -n infected -l False
  --flow="{srcip=10.0.0.1}" -a

127.0.0.1-p 50001
```

Figure 5.18 illustrates some controller's output informing that the last event was received and the forwarding policy changed to forward the traffic towards host "h2" (policy identity).

From Figure 5.19, it is possible to conclude that host "h1" is now receiving a response from host "h2" itself.

```
64 bytes from 10.0.0.3 icmp_req=1 ttl=64 time=115 ms
64 bytes from 10.0.0.3 icmp_req=2 ttl=64 time=112 ms

--- 10.0.0.2 ping statistics ---
2 packets transmitted, 2 received, 0% packet loss, time 1002ms
rtt min/avg/mdev = 112.492/114.106/115.720/1.614 ms
mininet> h1 ping -c 2 h2
PING 10.0.0.2 (10.0.0.2) 56(84) bytes of data.
64 bytes from 10.0.0.2 icmp_req=1 ttl=64 time=113 ms
64 bytes from 10.0.0.2 icmp_req=2 ttl=64 time=59.5 ms

--- 10.0.0.2 ping statistics ---
2 packets transmitted, 2 received, 0% packet loss, time 1001ms
rtt min/avg/mdev = 59.529/86.713/113.897/27.184 ms
mininet>
```

FIGURE 5.19   ICMP traffic is reaching again host h2.

At the final point, we finish our current evaluation of the intelligent IDS/IPS system. This is considered as an important feature to be incorporated in Big Data scenarios once it facilitates the identification and solving of some attacks that a distributed Big Data architecture (in different phases of the Big Data life cycle – from data capture to data processing and consumption) can suffer.

5.8 BIG DATA SECURITY: FUTURE DIRECTIONS

This chapter emphasizes on some of the most important aspects of security and privacy challenges that affect Big Data working environment. Although the information security practices, methodologies and tools to ensure the security and privacy of the Big Data ecosystem already exist, the particular characteristics of Big Data make them ineffective if they are not used in an integrated manner. This chapter shows some solutions to the challenges generally facing in Big Data environment, but it does not provide finite or accurate solutions for the problem. It rather points to contribute some directions and technologies to solve some of the most relevant and challenging Big Data security and privacy issues.

Next, two different use cases were presented. Both of the use cases present some directions that contribute to solving part of the large Big Data security and privacy puzzle. In the first use case, it was presented an approach that tries solving security and privacy issues on social network's UGC. In this approach, an open and interoperable rights management system was proposed as a way to improve the privacy of users that share content over social networks. The processes described show how the rights management system puts the end-users on the control of their own UGC, and how they prevent abuses from either other users or the social network platform itself. The second use case presented the capabilities offered by SDN in increasing the ability to collect statistical data from the network and allowing controller applications for programming and forwarding the devices, which are the powerful and smart security enforcement techniques like active security (Hand, Ton, & Keller 2013). This novel security methodology proposes a novel feedback loop to improve the control of defense mechanisms of a networked infrastructure, and is centered around five core capabilities: protect, sense, adjust, collect and counter (Kreutz et al. 2014). In this perspective, active security provides a centralized programming interface that simplifies the integration of mechanisms for detecting attacks by (i) collecting data from diverse sources (to identify attacks with more assertiveness), (ii) converging to a consistent policy configuration for the security appliances and (iii) enforcing countermeasures to block or minimize the effect of such attacks. Previous aspects were partially covered by our IDS/IPS case study, but notably need to be further developed and are an important contribution to the security and privacy of Big Data ecosystem.

It is clear throughout the chapter that some important steps are considered for solving Big Data security and privacy issues and still a long road to move ahead. In the conclusion of this chapter, we would like to refer to some interesting topics where the research community could work actively to develop new Big Data security and privacy solutions.

Research challenges in this Big Data ecosystem range from the data creation (and the Big Data sources – devices) to data storage and transportation, data transformation and processing and finally data usage. To support this life cycle, a high-capacity and highly distributed architecture will be necessary, exposed to a hostile environment subject to all kinds of attacks. The SDN approach as proposed in this chapter is a possible solution to counter these threats; however, further research needs to be conducted, like concerns to the automatic adaptation of switching and behavior-based security policies (Chen, Jorgen, & Yuan 2011, Dohi & Uemura 2012).

There are research challenges on maintaining end-to-end data security and privacy to ensure that they should not be revealed in clear to unauthorized parties during any point of Big Data life cycle. In moving from data to programs, there are various techniques for protecting privacy in browsing, searching and social interaction methods. Some more research needs to be conducted on the processing of encrypted data and privacy protection in the context of both computer programs and web-based systems.

More research challenges in the Big Data area include developing techniques to perform transparent computations over encrypted data with multiple keys, from multiple sources and multiple users. In terms of research, it would be challenging to study and develop ways to delegate limited functions over encrypted data, so that third parties can analyze it. All the aspects related to key management, authorization delegation and management of rights are topics that require further research in this field. Trust is everything when considering secure and private-aware systems. In particular, in the case of Big Data, a trustworthy environment should be established for most of the scenarios (healthcare, assisted living, SCADA systems and many others). It is a research direction challenging terms to achieve this environment. Trusting applications that are capable of querying and processing Big Data and extracting knowledge from it, and trusting devices that collect all the data from multiple sources, constitute a basic security requirement. Generating and establishing trust among the end-users, the devices (IoT) and the applications is a hot research topic for the coming years.

On what concerns Big Data, these research challenges represent only the tip of the iceberg about the problems that still need to be studied and solved on the development of secure and privacy-aware Big Data ecosystem.

5.9 FINAL RECOMMENDATIONS

Following are some key recommendations in helping to make fewer effects on security risks and threats identified in the Big Data ecosystem.

1. Select the products and vendors that have back proven experience and have similar-scale deployments.
   Request for vendor references for large-scale deployments (similar in size of your organization) that are running the security controls under consideration for at least 1 year.

2. **Main pillars:** Accountability, centric balancing network, centric access control and data-centric security are absolutely critical in achieving a good overall trustworthy security posture.

3. Data-centric security, such as label security or cell-level security for sensitive data, is preferred. Both of these security types are integrated into the data or application code rather than adding data security after the fact.

4. Use data reduction, data masking or tokenization at the time of ingestion, or use data services with granular controls to access Hadoop. Externalize data security, if possible.

5. Data management tools such as OSS Apache Falcon, Cloudera Navigator or the Zettaset Orchestrator are used to harness the log and audit. This helps achieve data provenance in the long run.

REFERENCES

Advantech. 2013. Enhancing Big Data Security. Retrieved from www.advantech. com.tw/nc/newsletter/whitepaper/big_data/big_data.pdf.

Agrawal, D., Das, S., & El Abbadi, A. 2011. Big data and cloud computing. *In Proceedings of the 14th International Conference on Extending Database Technology - EDBT/ICDT '11*, New York, ACM Press (p. 530). doi: 10.1145/1951365.1951432.

Chen, P., Jorgen, B., & Yuan, Y. 2011. Software behavior based trusted attestation. *In Proceedings of 3rd International Conference on Measuring Technology and Mechatronics Automation, ICMTMA 2011* (Vol. 3, pp. 298–301). doi: 10.1109/ICMTMA.2011.645.

Chen, X., & Shi, S. 2009. A literature review of privacy research on social network sites. *In MINES'09. International Conference on Multimedia Information Networking and Security*, Shanghai, China (Vol. 1, pp. 93–97).

Cloud Security Alliance. 2013. Expanded Top Ten Security and Privacy Challenges. Retrieved from https://downloads.cloudsecurityalliance.org/ initiatives/bdwg/Expanded_Top_Ten_Big_Data_Security_and_Privacy_ Challenges.pdf.

CTL. 2014. Computation Tree Logic. Retrieved July 17, 2014, from http:// en.wikipedia.org/wiki/Computation_tree_logic.

DARPA. 2014. Mining and Understanding Software Enclaves (Muse). Retrieved August 03, 2014, from www.darpa.mil/Our_Work/I2O/Programs/Mining_ and_Understanding_Software_Enclaves_(MUSE).aspx.

De Cristofaro, E., Soriente, C., Tsudik, G., & Williams, A. 2012. Hummingbird: Privacy at the time of twitter. *In 2012 IEEE Symposium on Security and Privacy (SP)*, San Francisco, CA (pp. 285–299).

Demchenko, Y., Ngo, C., de Laat, C., Membrey, P., & Gordijenko, D. 2014. Big security for big data: Addressing security challenges for the big data infrastructure. In: Jonker, W. & Petković, M. (Eds.) *Secure Data Management* (pp. 76–94). Springer International Publishing. Retrieved from http://link. springer.com/chapter/10.1007/978-3-319-06811-4_13.

Dohi, T., & Uemura, T. 2012. An adaptive mode control algorithm of a scalable intrusion tolerant architecture. *Computer and System Sciences*, 78, 1751–1754.

Feamster, N. 2014. Software Defined Networking. Retrieved August 02, 2014, from www.coursera.org/course/sdn.

Gentry, C. 2009. A fully homomorphic encryption scheme. Stanford University. Retrieved from http://cs.au.dk/~stm/local-cache/gentry-thesis.pdf.

Gentry, C. 2010. Computing arbitrary functions of encrypted data. *Communications of the ACM*. doi: 10.1145/1666420.1666444.

Goldwasser, S., Gordon, S. D., Goyal, V., Jain, A., Katz, J., Liu, F.-H., … Zhou, H.-S. 2014. Multiinput functional encryption. *In Advances in Cryptology - EUROCRYPT 2014: 33rd Annual International Conference on the Theory and Applications of Cryptographic Techniques*, Copenhagen, Denmark (pp. 578–602).

Gross, R., & Acquisti, A. 2005. Information revelation and privacy in online social networks. *In Proceedings of the 2005 ACM Workshop on Privacy in the Electronic Society*, Alexandria, VA (pp. 71–80).

Hand, R., Ton, M., & Keller, E. 2013. Active security. *In Proceedings of the Twelfth ACM Workshop on Hot Topics in Networks: HotNets-XII*, New York, ACM Press (pp. 1–7).

Hasan, O., Habegger, B., Brunie, L., Bennani, N., & Damiani, E. 2013. A discussion of privacy challenges in user profiling with big data techniques: The EEXCESS use case. *IEEE International Congress on Big Data*, Seattle, WA (pp. 25–30).

HP. 2014. Internet of Things Research Study (p. 4). http://fortifyprotect.com/HP_IoT_Research_Study.pdf.

IBM. 2014. IBM Big Data Platform: Bringing Big Data to the Enterprise. 2014 July. CT000.

IDC. 2012. Big Data in 2020. www.emc.com/leadership/digitaluniverse/2012iview/big-data-2020.htm.

Juels, A., & Oprea, A. 2013. New approaches to security and availability for cloud data. *Communications of the ACM*, 56(2), 64.

Jutla, D. N., Bodorik, P., & Ali, S. 2013. Engineering privacy for big data apps with the unified modeling language. *IEEE International Congress on Big Data 2013*, Santa Clara, CA (pp. 38–45).

Kim, C., Jin, M.-H., Kim, J., & Shin, N. 2012. User perception of the quality, value, and utility of user generated content. *Journal of Electronic Commerce Research*, 13(4), 305–319.

Kindervag, J., Balaouras, S., Hill, B., & Mak, K. 2012. *Control and Protect Sensitive Information in the Era of Big Data*. Academic Press: Cambridge, MA.

Kindervag, J., Wang, C., Balaouras, S., & Coit, L. 2011. *Applying Zero Trust To The Extending Enterprise*. Academic Press: Cambridge, MA.

Kreutz, D., Ramos, F. M. V., Verissimo, P., Rothenberg, C. E., Azodolmolky, S., & Uhlig, S. 2014. Software-defined networking: A comprehensive survey, 49. *Networking and Internet Architecture*. http://arxiv.org/abs/1406.0440.

Lindell, Y., & Pinkas, B. 2002. Privacy preserving data mining. *Journal of Cryptology*, 15(3), 177–206.

Luo, H., Lin, Y., Zhang, H., & Zukerman, M. 2013. Preventing DDoS attacks by identifier/locator separation. *IEEE Network*, 27(6), 60–65.

Marques, J., & Serrão, C. 2013a. Improving content privacy on social networks using open digital rights management solutions. *Procedia Technology*, 9, 405–410.

Marques, J., & Serrão, C. 2013b. Improving user content privacy on social networks using rights management systems. *Annals of Telecommunications: Annales Des Télécommunications*, 69(1–2), 37–45.

McKenzie, P. J., Burkell, J., Wong, L., Whippey, C., Trosow, S. E., & McNally, M. B. 2012, June 6. http://firstmonday.org/ojs/index.php/fm/article/view/3912/3266.

Michael, K., & Miller, K. W. 2013. Big data: New opportunities and new challenges [guest editors' introduction]. *Computer*, 46(6), 22–24.

MIT. 2014. Big Data Privacy Workshop, Advancing the State of the Art in Technology and Practice. http://web.mit.edu/bigdatapriv/images/MITBigDataPrivacyWorkshop2014_final05142014.pdf.

Monsanto, C., Reich, J., Foster, N., Rexford, J., & Walker, D. 2013. Composing software-defined networks. *Proceedings of the 10th USENIX Conference on Networked Systems Design and Implementation*, Lombard, IL (pp. 1–14). http://dl.acm.org/citation.cfm?id=2482626.2482629\nhttp://www.frenetic-lang.org/pyretic/.

NIST. 2014. Framework for Improving Critical Infrastructure Cyber security. www.nist.gov/cyberframework/upload/cybersecurity-framework-021214-final.pdf.

NuSMV. 2014. An overview of NuSMV. Retrieved July 23, 2014, http://nusmv.fbk.eu/NuSMV/.

Okhravi, H., Hobson, T., Bigelow, D., & Streilein, W. 2014. Finding focus in the blur of moving target techniques. *IEEE Security and Privacy*, 12(2), 16–26.

OWASP. 2014. OWASP Internet of Things Top Ten Project. Retrieved August 05, 2014, from www.owasp.org/index.php/OWASP_Internet_of_Things_Top_Ten_Project.

Popa, R., & Redfield, C. 2011. CryptDB: Protecting Confidentiality with Encrypted Query Processing, pp. 85–100.

Popa, R., & Redfield C. 2012. CryptDB: Processing queries on an encrypted data-base. *Communication*, 55, 103.

Pyretic Language. 2014. https://github.com/freneticlang/pyretic/wiki/Language-BasicsPython.

Python Language. 2014. www.python.org/.

Rivera, J. & van der Meulen, R. 2014. Gartner Says the Internet of Things Will Transform the Data Center. www.gartner.com/newsroom/id/2684915.

Rodríguez, E., Rodríguez, V., Carreras, A., & Delgado, J. 2009. A digital rights management approach to privacy in online social networks. *Workshop on Privacy and Protection in Web-based Social Networks (ICAIL'09)*, Barcelona.

Serrão, C. 2008. IDRM - Interoperable Digital Rights Management: Interoperability Mechanisms for Open Rights Management Platforms. Universitat Politècnica de Catalunya. http://repositorio-iul.iscte.pt/handle/10071/1156.

Serrão, C., Dias, M., & Delgado, J. 2005. Web-services to manage and control access to multimedia content. *ISWS05-The 2005 International Symposium on Web Services and Applications*, Las Vegas, NV.

Serrão, C., Neves, D., Barker, T., & Balestri, M. 2003. Open SDRM: An open and secure digital rights management solution. *In Proceedings of the IADIS International Conference e-Society*, Lisbon.

Serrão, C., Rodriguez, E., & Delgado, J. 2011. Approaching the rights management interoperability problem using intelligent brokerage mechanisms. *Computer Communications*, 34(2), 129–139.

Tankard, C. 2012. Big data security. *Network Security*, 2012(7), 5–8.

Thomas S. A. 2000. *SSL & TLS Essentials: Securing the Web (Pap/Cdr., p. 224)*. Wiley: Hoboken, NJ.

Van Dijk, M., Gentry, C., Halevi, S., & Vaikuntanathan, V. 2010. Fully homomorphic encryption over the integers. *In Annual International Conference on the Theory and Applications of Cryptographic Techniques*, Berlin, Germany (pp. 24–43).

CHAPTER 6

Data Science and Big Data Analytics

Ananta Charan Ojha

Centurion University of Technology and Management

Subhendu Kumar Pani

Orissa Engineering College (OEC)
Biju Patnaik University of Technology (BPUT)

CONTENTS

6.1 OBJECTIVE

With the growth of social media, connectivity, ubiquitous computing, Internet of Things, ambient intelligence and above all digital economy, the field of big data has emerged as a challenge as well as an opportunity for many organizations. While big data stores a lot of business opportunities, how to make it useful for the organization is rather challenging. In this context, embracing data science becomes more pertinent for the organization. With the advent of big data, the importance and popularity of data science are accelerating.

This chapter provides a compressive introduction to data science and big data analytics. It elaborates the data analytics life cycle and delves into the methods and techniques used in data science. It also introduces the relevant processing models of big data.

6.2 INTRODUCTION

The popularity of the Internet and the World Wide Web has been tremendous in the past decade or so. The Internet and the World Wide Web have become a huge source of universal information for people of all ages and walks of life. Two amazing innovations, namely, mobile phones and social web, have changed the way people get connected. There is an exponential growth of smartphones and mobile applications around the world. Mobile technology unfolded the usage of the Internet to a much greater reach. People find a new way to communicate using the social web. The user base in social networking websites such as Facebook, Twitter and LinkedIn remains incredible [11,18]. Using blogging, people across the globe are expressing and publishing their ideas and opinions like never before. E-commerce has been flourished over the last two decades and able to attract online shoppers. The growth of e-commerce industry is triggered by increased penetration of smartphones and usage of the Internet.

Today, the Internet has established itself as a powerful platform to do business and communicate with others. It continues to be the most economical and appealing medium for masses. Almost any business can reach a very large market directly, fast and economically no matter what the size or location of the business is.

Furthermore, there has been a massive deployment of IT infrastructure across organizations due to intense pressure emanating from customer choice and business competition. In the past decade, it has been a trend that many organizations implemented ERP (Enterprise Resource Planning), CRM (Customer Relationship Management) and SCM (Supply Chain Management) solutions as a part of their strategy to improve the overall business performance and get a competitive edge. The organizational information systems of different types generate huge data as part of the operational activities of the business. Not only the transactions made by customers with the business are captured in the deployed IT systems, but also customer interactions, error messages, application usage logs and much more can be captured as needed.

Data is ubiquitous; it is on-the-Internet and off-the-Internet on the mobile phones and the organizational systems. Users of these systems move from information consumers to data producers during their interactions. All of these systems generate massive data every minute creating data explosion. While many see the phenomena as a challenge in terms of handling the data explosion, others foresee a huge opportunity in terms of data analytics for organizations and their business. The data generated on these systems can be collected and analyzed to discern patterns and trends, and provide valuable insights for organizations.

6.2.1 What Is Big Data?

Big data is ubiquitous and invades almost every industry and organization today [3,4]. It originates from a variety of sources, internal and external to the organization. It can be interactions and transactions captured in organizational IT systems, social media, mobile devices and sensor networks. To understand big data, one needs to recognize its varied characteristics [5]. Big data is characterized by using several V's, which may be categorized into primary and secondary based on their association and importance (Figure 6.1) [1,2]. The primary V's are volume, variety and velocity, while the secondary V's are veracity, value, variability, volatility and visualization, which are explained further as follows:

Volume: The most important characteristic of big data is volume. It refers to the scale of data generation. The amount of data generated is so huge that it makes the traditional methods inefficient to store and process the data [7].

Variety: In addition to the conventional data format, big data comes in the form of images, video and audio streams, satellite signals, GPS data, natural language texts, etc. As a result, big data comprises different types of data such as structured, semi-structured and unstructured [9].

Velocity: It refers to the speed at which the data is generated and/or processed. For example, in Twitter on average, more than 360,000 tweets are sent per minute. Internet users generate about 2.6 quintillion bytes of data daily. On average, Google processes over 40,000 searches per second. The speed of big data generation and processing is mind-boggling.

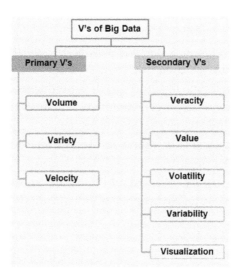

FIGURE 6.1   Characteristics of big data.

Veracity: It refers to the reliability of the data, credibility of its source and trustworthiness of its generation. It affects the quality of big data [10]. For example, satellite signals are affected when faced with obstacles on the way. Similarly, when it comes to data generated on the buying habits of customers in different shopping malls, one may question on the methodology adopted to collect the data.

Value: It is another important characteristic of big data [12], which determines the utility of the data. If there is no added business value that can be derived from the data, then there is no point in embarking on it.

Volatility: It refers to the currency of data. Due to velocity and volume, data currency is very important. If the data gets older very quickly and its relevance diminishes with time, then it may not be appropriate to keep the data live, which inflicts cost and performance issues in processing systems.

Variability: Variability in big data refers to inconsistency resulted when data is captured from multiple and disparate sources. It can be in the form of anomaly or outlier in the data. Variability in data needs careful preprocessing.

Visualization: Data visualization is an important aspect in data analytics. Considering the volume, variety and velocity of data, it may be difficult to visualize the data using available visualization tools and techniques.

6.2.2 What Is Data Science?

Data science is an interdisciplinary field that deals with a methodical approach to process large volumes of data both structured and unstructured in nature. The main objective is to analyze the data in order to uncover hidden patterns and extract actionable insights from it for better managerial decision-making in an organization. Data science has been used in diverse areas such as business and finance, marketing, risk management, operations and planning, disease diagnosis and health care, agriculture, fraud detection, crime investigation, image and speech recognition, gaming, virtual reality, weather and environmental studies, space and defense applications to name a few.

Data science is not an entirely new discipline; rather, it is mashup of several existing disciplines such as data mining and knowledge

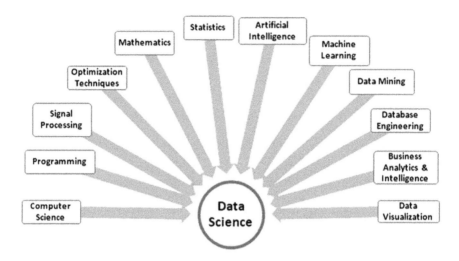

FIGURE 6.2   Major disciplines contributing to data science.

discovery, business intelligence, data analytics, artificial intelligence (AI) and machine learning, natural language processing and information retrieval, database technologies, software engineering, mathematics and statistics, among others (Figure 6.2). It is an umbrella term for many such disciplines, which make data processing more systematic than ever before. With the growth of big data and significant developments in the areas of machine learning and scalable computing infrastructures, the popularity of data science has gone up. Data science with its methodical approach to data analysis is very useful for organizational decision-making. It has a lot of potentials to solve complex organizational problems effectively.

6.2.3 What Is Data Analytics?

Data analytics is a broad term that encompasses diverse types of data analysis using extensive mathematical and statistical methods, techniques and tools to reveal hidden knowledge in data for better organization decisions. It can be qualitative data analysis or quantitative data analysis. Data analytics supports a wide range of organizational use cases [19]. For example, an e-commerce company may analyze browsing patterns of visitors on its website to identify potential buyers for its products or services. A mobile phone service provider may analyze the service usage habits of its customers in order to predict potential churn and take necessary measures to prevent it. Similarly, a manufacturing company

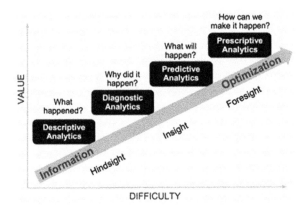

FIGURE 6.3   Gartner analytic ascendancy model. (Source: Gartner, March 2012.)

may record its product's demand that varies on time and optimizes its production schedule. Therefore, data analytics can be divided into four basic types. Gartner analytics ascendancy model illustrates these analytics with respect to the level of difficulty and value associated with them (Figure 6.3). However, a linear relationship between difficulty and value depicted in the model is a mere simplification of reality for illustration purposes only.

6.2.3.1 Descriptive Analytics

Descriptive analytics is the simplest and most common form of analytics used across organizations. It summarizes the data on past events and produces metrics and measures of the business that has happened for easier interpretation. Descriptive analytics provides hindsight and explains what happened in the past. However, it fails to explain why it happened, for example, the daily sales volume of different items in a retail store, the total value of the sales and the number of customers attributed to the sales.

6.2.3.2 Diagnostic Analytics

Diagnostic analytics digs deeper into the metrics and measures when a positive or negative issue arises. It provides insights and answers question "why did it happen?" For example, if there is a higher volume or lower volume of sales in a period, then it perhaps explains the reason thereof by providing cause–effect relationship.

6.2.3.3 Predictive Analytics

While descriptive analytics and diagnostic analytics explain the past, predictive analytics estimates the future event based on the historical data. It provides foresight of a business and answers the question "what will happen?" The accuracy of prediction depends on the quality of past data and the two former analytics types. For example, based on the historical sales data, the retail store can forecast demand and manage its stock level in order to avoid the consequences of the stock-out situation.

6.2.3.4 Prescriptive Analytics

The last one in the ladder is prescriptive analytics, which provides more value to the organization than other analytics types. It is an advanced form of analytics that requires complex techniques. It not only predicts the likelihood of an event that may take place in the future, but also suggests the course of action to make the event happen if it is favorable or to prevent the event if it is not favorable. For example, a taxi driver gets the best route out of the routes available from a source to destination considering several factors such as the distance of each route, the speed at which the taxi can travel and the traffic condition at that point of time. The prescriptive analytics utilizes hindsight, insight and foresight of the previous three analytics and recommends the best course of action for a situation to happen.

6.2.4 Data Analytics Process

Data analytics process comprises several activities to carry out a data analytics project. While no industry standard process model exists, the major stages of an analytics project are presented here (Figure 6.4).

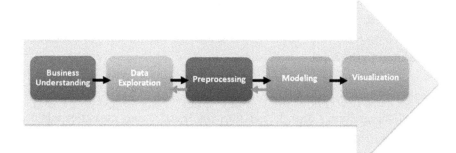

FIGURE 6.4   Data analytics process.

6.2.4.1 Business Understanding

Every data analytics project begins with an outline of the project, key objectives and outcomes. The data scientists need to identify and understand the business problem, and decide the type of analytics approach to be followed to address the problem.

6.2.4.2 Data Exploration

Next, the project team decides the data requirements based on the chosen analytics approach. Data is gathered from internal and external sources. An understanding of the data in terms of its adequacy and quality is gained keeping in mind the nature of analytics to be performed. A descriptive statistics and visualization of the data are obtained to understand the data.

6.2.4.3 Preprocessing

Preprocessing stage encompasses all activities that make the data suitable for modeling. Data gathered from multiple sources need to be integrated. Sometimes data values need to be transformed from one form to another using normalization and aggregation. Data needs to be cleaned to fill missing values and remove duplicate instances. Feature selection may be carried out to deal with the curse of dimensionality. Data preparation is the most time-consuming step in the analytics process, which may be iterative with its preceding and following stages.

6.2.4.4 Modeling

Once the data is prepared and made suitable, model building activities start. There are several modeling algorithms available. Depending upon the type of analytics and nature of data, one or more algorithms may be used. Data may be split randomly into training dataset and test dataset. A model is trained using the training dataset and tested using the test dataset. Several evaluation metrics depicting statistical significance are considered to evaluate the model performance. The model parameters may be tuned to produce the desired result in order to address the business problem. Thus, model building and evaluation activities may be performed iteratively.

6.2.4.5 Data Visualization

Once the model is tuned and the desired results are achieved, data visualization is performed to present the results of the analytics process.

It enables decision makers to understand the analytics easily. Using interactive visualization, the decision maker can drill down into a deeper level of the data to gain foresight of the business.

6.3 TECHNIQUES FOR DATA ANALYTICS

A host of techniques exist for different stages of data analytics process. Some select techniques that are used in preprocessing and modeling stages are presented.

6.3.1 Techniques in Preprocessing Stage

Most of the time, the raw data gathered is not suitable for analysis in its original form. Data quality is very critical for data analytics. Poor quality of data reduces the quality of data analytics. Therefore, several preprocessing techniques are used to improve the quality of data.

6.3.1.1 Data Cleaning

Data cleaning deals with incomplete data that contains missing values or attributes, noisy data that may be due to errors and outliers, and inconsistent data that may be due to different forms of the same data. Data must be cleaned before building any model. With a properly cleaned dataset, learning algorithms can provide impressive insights from the data.

Dealing with missing values: Missing values in data cannot simply be ignored as some learning algorithms are very sensitive to them. There are two broad approaches to deal with missing values: dropping and filling. In dropping, the data instances that contain missing attribute values are removed from the dataset. However, dropping is suboptimal because the instances may be informative from other attributes point of view, and dropping instances result in loss of information. In filling, the missing values are filled from other instances. For example, a missing value can be filled with the mean value of the attribute or a predicted value using a learning algorithm. In WEKA machine learning tool, several filters are available for this purpose.

Outlier detection: An outlier is an extreme value of an attribute that deviates from the overall data pattern of the same attribute in the dataset. Since outliers cause learning problems in many algorithms, they must be removed, thus helping in improving the performance of a model. However, there must be a legitimate reason to remove outliers. Because an outlier may be an error in the data due to faulty data capture, it can also be a real value showing variability in the data that indicates a novelty. Several techniques such as Z-score, interquartile range, DBSCAN (density-based spatial clustering of applications with noise) and Isolation Forests exist to deal with an outlier.

6.3.1.2 Data Transformation

Raw data must be transformed to a suitable format so that machine learning algorithms can be applied effectively for analytic modeling. Data transformation deals with normalization, aggregation, attribute construction and discretization.

Normalization: Data normalization refers to transforming the data values of an attribute to fall within a specified scale satisfying a particular property. Techniques such as min-max, Z-score and decimal scaling are common for normalization. In min-max normalization, the following formula is used to transform an original data value to a new value that falls within a specified range:

$$v' = \frac{v - \min_A}{\max_A - \min_A}\left(\text{new\_max}_A - \text{new\_min}_A\right) + \text{new\_min}_A$$

where v is the original data value; $\min_A$ and $\max_A$ are the minimum and maximum values of an attribute A; v' is the new value; new_max_A and new_min_A are the maximum and minimum values of a specified range into which the original data values to be transformed.

In Z-score, the data values of an attribute are transformed into a scale with a mean of zero and a standard deviation of one. The following formula is used for the purpose:

$$v' = \frac{v - \mu}{\sigma}$$

where v is the original data value; v' is the new value; μ and σ are the mean and standard deviation data value of the attribute, respectively.

Similarly, in decimal scaling, the data values of an attribute are transformed to new values by moving their decimal points using the following formula such that the new values are always less than one:

$$v' = \frac{v}{10^n}$$

where v is the original data value; v' is the new value; n is the number of digits in the original data value.

Aggregation: In data aggregation, summarization is needed to provide a high-level view of the data. For example, data gathered per day can be aggregated into weeks, months and years; similarly, city-wise data can be aggregated into regions, states and countries.

Attribute construction: Sometimes two or more attributes are combined into a single attribute. The new attribute thus created can capture important information in a dataset more efficiently than the original attributes. For example, population data containing city, area and population as attributes can be transformed into city and density (i.e., area and population combined).

Discretization: It is used to transform a continuous attribute into an ordinal attribute. The range of the continuous attribute is divided into multiple intervals (or bins), and interval labels are used to replace actual data values. For example, numeric values of the attribute age can be replaced with child, young, middle-aged, senior-citizen, etc; a continuous attribute height can be given values like short, medium and tall. Many learning algorithms perform better when attribute values are small in number.

6.3.1.3 Dimensionality Reduction

Both the number of attributes and the number of instances in a dataset constitute a dimension of data. Dataset with high dimension is occasionally a curse to data analytics. High-dimensional space is complex and hard to discern patterns. Machine learning algorithms often take a long time and memory to process the data. High-dimensional data should be reduced for an effective application of sensitive algorithms.

Feature subset selection: Often a dataset contains several attributes that sometime provide redundant information or are not very significant from an analytics point of view. These irrelevant attributes must be removed during data preprocessing stage. There are different algorithms that evaluate the attributes in a dataset based on their worthiness with respect to the target class and produce an optimal subset of attributes. For example, in WEKA machine learning tool, algorithms such as CfsSubsetEval, CorrelationAttributeEval and InfoGainAttributeEval are used for the purpose.

Principal components analysis (PCA): It is one of the most popular techniques for dimensionality reduction. PCA reduces the number of attributes by searching a lower-dimensional space that can best represent the dataset. Dimensionality reduction is accomplished by choosing enough eigenvectors to account for a high percentage (usually 96% or more) of the variance in the original data.

Sampling: Sampling is used to select a representative subset of instances from the dataset for analysis, which approximately holds the same property of the original dataset. It reduces the size of the data and makes the algorithm learn faster. There are different types of sampling such as simple random sampling, stratified sampling and progressive sampling.

6.3.2 Techniques in Modeling Stage

During modeling stage, one or more techniques are used to learn from the dataset and find a model fit for it. These learning techniques are broadly classified as supervised and unsupervised. In a supervised technique, the algorithm learns from a set of examples called training data. Each instance in the training dataset contains an output for a given set of inputs. Once a data model is learned, it is used to predict the output of a new set of inputs. On the other hand, an unsupervised learning algorithm learns from a dataset wherein an instance does not contain an output for a set of inputs. The learning algorithm uses its traits to form groups out of the data. All instances in a data group are similar to one another.

6.3.2.1 Regression

Regression is an important supervised learning technique for analytics modeling of data. Simple regression shows the causal relationship between two variables: One is designated as the independent variable and the other is the dependent variable. Unlike correlation that shows the degree of relationship between two undesignated variables, regression shows the cause–effect relationship between the dependent and independent variables. Further, regression goes beyond correlation and predicts the dependent variable when the independent variable is known. There are several types of regression techniques, which differ in terms of the type of dependent variables, number of independent variables and shape of the regression line. Some of the common regression techniques are outlined here.

Linear regression: It is the simplest and most widely used predictive modeling technique. The variables used in the model are assumed to be completely linear. The dependent variable is continuous, while the independent variable(s) can be continuous or discrete. When only one independent variable and one dependent variable form the regression model, it is called the univariate linear regression model. However, the more general form of the regression model is multivariate (or multiple) linear regression where multiple independent variables (called features) form the model represented by the following equation:

$$Y = a + b_1 X_1 + b_2 X_2 + \cdots + b_n X_n,$$

where "Y" is the dependent variable, "X_n" are the independent variables, "b_n" are the regression coefficients, and "a" is the intercept.

Linear regression is intuitive, fast and easy to model when the relationship among variables is not very complex. However, linear regression is very sensitive to outliers that terribly affect the regression line and eventually the prediction. When the independent variables are highly correlated with each other (or multicollinearity), it becomes difficult to know which independent variable is the most important to predict the dependent variable.

Polynomial regression: In polynomial regression, the regression equation is represented using a polynomial function of independent variables. The relationship between the dependent variable and independent variables is nonlinear. Thus, a polynomial regression equation using the polynomial of degree k in one independent variable can be written as:

$$Y = a + b_1 X + b_2 X^2 + \cdots + b_n X^n$$

Multiple independent variables (or features) can be added to the equation when multiple polynomial regression is considered. However, it should be noted that a large number of unnecessary features or polynomial of a higher degree may lead to the problem of over-fitting.

Logistic regression: It is used to predict the dependent variable, which is binary in nature (e.g., 0/1, true/false). Independent variables can be continuous or binary. Logistic regression can have a linear or nonlinear relationship between the dependent and independent variables. It requires large training dataset for model building and assumes no multicollinearity. All the independent variables should be significant to avoid the problems of over-fitting and under-fitting. Logistic regression is widely used for classification problems. When the dependent variable is multi-class (i.e., more than two values), logistic regression is called multinomial logistic regression.

6.3.2.2 Classification

Data classification is generally defined as the process of organizing data by related categories so that it may be used and confined more efficiently.

On a fundamental level, the classification method makes data easier to locate and recover. Data classification is significantly compliant when it describes risk management and data security. Data classification includes tagging data to build it simply searchable and trackable. It also removes several duplications of data, which can lessen storage and backup costs while fasting up the search process. Although the classification procedure may sound very technical, it is a matter that should be realized by your organization's leadership.

6.3.2.3 Clustering

Cluster is a collection of similar objects that belongs to the alike class. Alternately, similar objects are collected in one cluster, and unrelated objects are collected in a new cluster [13]. Clustering can be derived from the most significant unsupervised learning problem; so, for each additional problem of this kind, it manages with finding a structure in a grouped data. In a simple definition, clustering is "the method of rearranging objects into clusters whose members are similar in some way".

A cluster is then a group of objects which are similar among them and are different than the other generated clusters [16]. The goal of clustering is to resolve the inherent grouping in a set of unrecognized data [17]. But it decides what comprises a quality clustering. It can be revealed that there is no supreme "best" criterion, which could be independent of the ultimate aim of the clustering. As a result, it is the user who should give this criterion. For example, it could be attracted in getting representatives for identical groups (data reduction), in discovering natural clusters, and in explaining their unidentified properties in extracting essential and suitable groupings or in discovering extraordinary data objects.

6.3.2.4 Association Rules

Association rule mining is a process that is meant to discover frequent patterns, correlations, associations or causal structures from datasets originating in different kinds of databases such as transactional databases, relational databases and other forms of data repositories. Given a group of transactions, association rule mining intends to get the rules, which allow us to forecast the occurrence of a particular item based on the incidences of the extra items in the transaction. Association rule mining is the data mining technique of finding the rules that may manage associations and underlying objects between groups of items. Thus, in a specified transaction with several items, it attempts to get the rules that manage how or

why such items are frequently bought together. For example, peanut but-
ter and jelly are often bought together. Association rules are frequently
essential to gratify a user-specified minimum support and a user-specified
minimum confidence at the same time.

6.3.2.5 Ensemble Learning

Ensemble learning is an important machine learning standard where
many learners are trained to resolve the same problem. On the contrary
to normal machine learning techniques that try to study one hypothesis
from training data, ensemble techniques try to build a set of hypotheses
and merge them to use. Ensembles include many learners who are generally called base learners. The generalization capability of an ensemble is
usually much accurate than that of base learners. In fact, ensemble learning is attractive because it can increase weak learners, who are somewhat
better than a random guess to burly learners, who can construct extremely
accurate predictions. So, "base learners" are also called "weak learners". It
is remarkable, although the majority of theoretical analyses are performed
on weak learners, base learners applied in practice are not essentially weak
since using not-so-weak base learners frequently results in improved performance. Base learners are generally produced from training data by a
base learning technique, which may be decision tree, neural network or
other types of machine learning techniques. The majority of ensemble
techniques apply a single base learning technique to generate uniform
base learners, but there are also some algorithms that use many learning techniques to generate heterogeneous learners. In the subsequent case,
there is no lone base learning method, and so, some people choose to call
the learners individual learners or component learners to base learners,
while the names "individual learners" and "component learners" can also
be applied for uniform base learners. It is hard to outline the starting point
of the account of ensemble methods since the fundamental idea of arrang-
ing many models has been in use for a long time, yet it is obvious that the
searing wave of research on ensemble learning since the 1990s should be
indebted much to two works.

6.3.2.6 Deep Learning

Deep learning is based on an AI function that replicates the mechanisms
of the human brain in processing data and generating patterns for the purpose of taking easy and accurate decision-making process. Deep learning
is a part of machine learning in AI that has networks having unsupervised

learning from data that is unstructured or unlabeled. Alternatively, it is recognized as a deep neural learning or deep neural network. Deep learning has developed hand-in-hand with the modern digital era, which has carried about an outburst of data in all types and from every region of the world. This data, also known as big data, is obtained from sources such as the Internet, social media search engines, e-commerce-raised areas and online cinemas, among others. This massive amount of data is voluntarily accessible and can be used through different applications like cloud computing.

On the other hand, the data, which is usually unstructured, is so huge that it could take decades for humans to understand it and extort related information.

6.3.2.7 Reinforcement Learning

Reinforcement learning is based on the type of machine learning. It is about taking appropriate action to maximize return in a specific situation. It is implemented by different pieces of software and machines to discover the best probable behavior or path it should get in a particular situation. Reinforcement learning is different than the supervised learning in a way that in supervised learning, the training data has the answer key with it so the model is trained with the right answer itself, whereas in reinforcement learning, there is no answer but the reinforcement agent chooses what to do to execute the specified task. Due to the lack of training dataset, it is valid to study from its experience.

6.3.2.8 Text Analysis

Text analysis is the process of parsing texts in order to derive machine-readable information from them. The main aim of text analysis is to form structured data out of freely available text content. The procedure consists of slicing and dicing heaps of unstructured, heterogeneous source documents into a simple form to manage and construct data pieces. Text analysis is very close to additional terms such as text mining, text analytics and information extraction. Text analysis and text mining are similar and used as synonyms. Information extraction is the name of the technical discipline behind text mining. All these vocabularies and terminologies are referred to partial natural language processing (NLP) where the ultimate goal is not to fully know the text, but rather to retrieve exact information from it in the most practical approach. Which means creating a good balance between the efforts required to build up and retain the analytical pipeline, its computational price and performance and its accuracy? The final is calculated with recall (extraction completeness), precision (quality of the extracted information) and jointly measures such as F-score.

6.3.2.9 Cross-Validation

Cross-validation, occasionally called rotation estimation or out-of-sample testing, is any of the different similar model validation methods for assessing how the outcome of a statistical analysis will generalize to an independent dataset. It is generally used in settings where the goal is to predict, and one needs to calculate how correctly a predictive model will execute in practice. In a prediction and forcastation problem, a model is generally given a dataset of known data on which training is run (training dataset), and a dataset of unknown data (or first seen data) against which the model is tested (testing dataset or validation set). The aim of cross-validation is to test the model's capability to predict novel data that was not used in calculating it, in order to flag problems like over-fitting or selection bias and to provide an insight on how the model will simplify to an independent dataset (i.e., an unidentified dataset, for instance, from a valid problem). A single round of cross-validation engages partitioning a sample of data into matching subsets, executing the analysis on one subset (known as the training set) and validating the study on the other subset (known as the validation set or testing set). To decrease variability, in many methods, various rounds of cross-validation are executed using various partitions, and the validation outcomes are merged (e.g., averaged) over the rounds to provide a calculation approximately of the model's predictive performance. So cross-validation merges (averages) measures of fitness in forcastation to derive a more perfect estimate of model prediction performance.

6.4 BIG DATA PROCESSING MODELS AND FRAMEWORKS

6.4.1 Map Reduce

Map Reduce representation model of data processing is developed by Google and Yahoo for their internal use. This data model is a retrieval model rather than a query model. The Internet or Web 2.0, if you like better, is really in progress with the LAMP stack of open-source software that any person could apply to get up a website: Linux (operating system), Apache (HTTP server), MySQL (database, but since it was acquired by Oracle, people are moving to the open-source version, MariaDB) and PHP,

Perl or Python for the application-based language. Apache and MySQL are now managed by Oracle Corporation and the open-source society doubts of them. There is an alike stack in the big data storage world called the SMAQ stack for storage, Map Reduce and query, rather than specific products per se. Like the LAMP stack, the tools that execute the layers of the SMAQ are generally open-source and run on hardware products. The functioning word here is "commodity" so that more shops can go to big data models.

This guides the clear question as to what the big data is. The finest answer I found is when the dimension of the data implicated in the project is a major anxiety for whatever reason. We seem for projects driven by the data, not computations or analysis of the data. The first web applications that hit this problem were web search engines. This creates sense; they were trying to operate with the increase of the web and not drop or leave out anything. Today, there are other performers on the web with size problems. The clear ones are social networks, multiplayer games and simulations, as well as big retailers and auction sites. But external of the web, mobile phones, sensors and other constant data flows can form petabytes of data. Google discovered the fundamental Map Reduce technique, but Yahoo really turned it into the Hadoop storage tools. As of this writing, the systems based on the Hadoop environment have a majority of the storage architectures. The query piece can be executed with Java because Hadoop is written in Java, but there are high-level query languages for these platforms (more on that later).

The Map Reduce part is significant of this model. Imagine a big open office with clerks sitting at their desks (commodity hardware), with heaps of catalogs in front of them. Positioning the catalogs on their desks is a huge process; it is unlike an SQL transaction model with interactive insert, update and delete query execution actions on the database.

Keeping with the workplace clerk's image, one time a day (or whatever temporal unit), the mail clerks put the day's catalogs on the clerk's desks. What the clerks do not see is that the mail room (data sources) has to be removed, filtered and sorted a bit before the mail obtained in the mail cart and distributed. The ETL (extract, transform, load) tools are from data warehousing effort in big data, too, but the data sources are not generally the clean, traditional structured ones that profitable data warehouses use. That is a whole topic in itself. But suppose we are ready for business. A boss at the front of the room shouts out the query: "Hey, get me a pair of red ballet flats!" to everyone, at the same time. Some of the clerks may realize that they do not contain shoe catalogs in the pile on their desk and will ignore the request. The rest of the clerks will pay instant attention and find looking through their catalogs. But what are they employed as a match? A human being knows that we request for a particular type and color of women's shoes.

A human being will look at a picture and realize it. A computer has to be programmed to do this, and that might consist of a weighted match score and not a yes/no result. The better the algorithm, the longer it takes to run and the more it prices in resources.

This is the mapping typed. The query has to be executed in parallel. In this resemblance, shouting out a query is enough, but the real world is not that easy. You must have tasks that can be performed independently of each other and yet merged into an alpha result. An additional mail clerk has to run down the rows of desks and pick up the strikes from the clerks, as they close at different rates. A number of clerks will have no matches, and we can omit them. A number of clerks will have a correct match to "red ballet flats" in their catalog; a number of clerks will have "ballet flats" or "red flats" near-matches.

6.4.2 Apache Frameworks

Apache Hadoop framework is a processing model that absolutely gives batch processing. Hadoop was the initial big data framework to get significant traction in the open-source community. Based on some papers and presentations by Google about how they were managing with terrific amounts of data at the time, Hadoop reapplied the techniques and component stack to create large-scale batch processing more reachable [8,14,15].

Contemporary versions of Hadoop are a collection of numerous components or layers that perform together to process batch data:

- **HDFS:** HDFS is the distributed file system layer that synchronizes storage and replication among the cluster nodes [6]. HDFS makes sure that data stays available in spite of predictable host failures. It is implemented at the source of data to keep intermediate processing results, and to persist the absolute calculated results.

- **YARN:** YARN, which abbreviated for Yet another Resource Negotiator, is to coordinate cluster components of the Hadoop stack. It is accountable for coordinating the underlying resources and scheduling tasks to be run. YARN makes it potential to run much more diverse workloads on a Hadoop cluster than was probable in earlier iterations by acting as a medium to the cluster resources.

6.5 SUMMARY

Big data analytics in an online environment is challenging because of its characteristics of 4Vs: volume, velocity, variety and veracity. There are various areas to optimize and advance its speed and scalability of big data analytics. Predictive analytics in big data with high-performance computing systems, machine learning and other strategies have been developed in the past and will maintain to be used heavily in the future computational applications. By applying these big data-related systems, engineers and scientists have been able to develop attractive design cars, airplanes and other vehicles. They have also been able to more accurately forecast daily weather as well as natural disaster. However, data science is an addition of mathematics and statistics that apply a variety of statistical tools and models combined in a machine or computer algorithm to cleanse dataset, analyze them and find out the latent patterns from a dataset. It helps in problem-solving; however, a specific algorithm requires to be fed to the computer along with the models to develop data and lessen it to predictive results. In any period of big data and data science, one thing is common for sure and that is data. So, all the researchers from these diverse fields belong to data mining, preprocessing and analyzing the data to present information about the behavior, attitude and perception of the consumers that assist the businesses to perform more efficiently and effectively. While big data is linked with large volumes of data, data analytics is applied to process the data to retrieve information and valuable knowledge with the aid of a tool recognized as data science.

REFERENCES

1. Gantz, J. and Reinsel, D., The digital universe in 2020: Big data bigger digital shadows and biggest growth in the far east, *IDC iView: IDC Analyze the future 2007*, 2012, 1–16, 2012.
2. Manyika, J. et al., *Big Data: The Next Frontier for Innovation Competition and Productivity*, San Francisco, CA: McKinsey Global Institute, pp. 1–137, 2011.
3. Economist, Drowning in Numbers: Digital Data Will Flood the Planet-and Help us Understand it Better, November 2011, [online] Available: www.economist.com/blogs/dailychart/2011/11/bigdata-0.

4. Noguchi, Y., *The Search for Analysts to Make Sense-of-Big-Data*, Washington, DC: National Public Radio, November 2011, [online] Available: www.npr.org/2011/11/30/14289306/the-search-foranalysts-to-make-%sense-of-big-data.

5. Kelly, J., Taming Big Data, 2013, [online] Available: http://wikibon.org/blog/taming-big-data/.

6. Howard, J. H. et al., Scale and performance in a distributed file system, *ACM Transactions on Computer Systems*, 6(1), 61–81, 1988.

7. Borkar, V., Carey, M. J., and Li, C., Inside big data management: Ogres onions or parfaits? *EDBT: 16th International Conference on Extending Database Technology*, Genoa, Italy, pp. 3–14, 2012.

8. Tatbul, N., Streaming data integration: Challenges and opportunities, *Proceeding of IEEE Second International Conference on Data Engineering Workshops (ICDEW)*, Long Beach, CA, pp. 166–168, March 2010.

9. Cooper, M. and Mell, P., Tackling Big Data, 2012, [online] Available: http://csrc.nist.gov/groups/SMA/forum/documents/june2012presentations/f%csm_june2012_cooper_mell.pdf.

10. O'Reilly Media, *Big Data Now: Current Perspectives from O'Reilly Radar*, Sebastopol, CA: O'Reilly Media, 2011.

11. Marche, S., Is Facebook making us lonely, *Atlantic*, 309(4), 0–9, 2012.

12. Dean, J., *Big Data, Data Mining, and Machine Learning: Value Creation for Business Leaders and Practitioners*, Hoboken, NJ: John Wiley & Sons, 2014.

13. Dean, J. and Ghemawat, S., Mapreduce: Simplified data processing on large clusters, *Communications of the ACM*, 61(1), 107–113, 2008.

14. Gama, J., *Knowledge Discovery from Data Streams*, Boca Raton, FL: CRC Press, 2010.

15. Gama, J., Rodrigues, P. P., and Sebastĩao, R., Evaluating algorithms that learn from data streams. *In Proceedings of the 2009 ACM Symposium on Applied Computing*, Honolulu, Hawaii, pp. 149–1600. ACM, 2009.

16. Gu, X., Angelov, P. P., Gutierrez, G., Iglesias, J. A., and Sanchis, A., Parallel computing teda for high frequency streaming data clustering. *In INNS Conference on Big Data*, Thessaloniki, Greece, pp. 238–263. Springer, 2016.

17. Guha, S., Meyerson, A., Mishra, N., Motwani, R., and O'Callaghan, L., Clustering data streams: Theory and practice, *IEEE Transactions on Knowledge and Data Engineering*, 16(3), 616–628, 2003.

18. Za'in, C., Pratama, M., Lughofer, E., and Anavatti, S. G., Evolving type-2 web news mining, *Applied Soft Computing*, 64, 200–220, 2017.

19. Borgman, C. L., The conundrum of sharing research data, *Journal of the American Society for Information Science and Technology*, 3, 1069–1078, 2012. doi: 10.1002/asi.2234.

CHAPTER 7

Awareness of Problems and Defies with Big Data Involved in Network Security Management with Revised Data Fusion-Based Digital Investigation Model

Sateesh Kumar Pradhan and
Satyasundara Mahapatra
Utkal University

Chandrakant Mallick
Biju Patnaik University of Technology

CONTENTS

7.1 INTRODUCTION

Digital forensics is the study of possible sources of digital information accumulated on computers, mobiles, game consoles and other various media storage devices for the purpose of significance to civil and criminal investigation [1–3]. The forensic examination of these digital data has to go through various steps such as identification, acquisition, preservation, examination and presentation so that documentation report containing potential pieces of evidence can be narrated before the court of law to penalize the cybercriminal and data can be protected. Forensic tools such as Forensic Tool Kit (FTK) [4] and ENCASE [5] are used following the steps of a well-approved digital investigation model to carry out this process [6,7]. The data offered by digital forensic investigation tools can habitually be disingenuous due to the dimensionality, intricacy and amount of the data presented [2,6,8]. Also, the scope of investigation and examination of evidence are limited to the examiners and investigators. Hence, it can raise challenges with the procreation nature of big data spreading heterogeneously [9,10].

The investigation and examination of various digital crimes require their analysis to be done with the already-approved digital forensic models and tools for better data management, data validation, data visualization and data dissemination keeping in mind the inherent and authentic value of the original evidence as well as proved digital media source [11,12]. The data generated by sectors such as businesses, public administrations, numerous industrial and not-to-profit sectors, and scientific research, social media sites, sensor networks, cyber-physical systems and Internet of Things is growing exponentially day-by-day [9,13]. The variety of data such as textual data to multimedia data being poured from different places anytime commonly coined as big data has become a budding data science paradigm for qualitative information mining leading to scientific discovery, data analytics as well as its digital crime examination and investigations [13]. The currently available digital forensic investigation models and tools are called conventional tools, which are dependent on signature-based analytics normally used in data cleaning and data separation [8,14]. But current trends of computer frauds and cybercrime demand organization and extraction of potential information of interest from the briskly cultivating large voluminous, variety and frequently changing data sets collected from heterogeneous and autonomous sources using possible fusion, mining, statistical and machine learning techniques [3,7,15–17].

The dramatic exponential growth of big data as well as the corresponding computer frauds and cybercrimes has gradually prolonged the research work in the field of digital forensics [10]. Digital evidence in the world of 0s and 1s is of probative value required to depict its value as a domain of discourse in the digital forensic community. There are many digital investigation models and approaches being developed to capture the digital evidence, but still its timely and accurate recovery, detection, aggregation, correlation and presentation are a distant dream. Much work has been done to digital investigation model as well as digital evidence but a comprehensive correlated and aggregated merging of data coming from different heterogeneous sources resulting from big data approach along with timely and accurate detection and analysis is the need of the hour [18].

So, with the exponential growth of big data in all sectors, this chapter attends to evaluate the techniques of data fusion with the intent of their application in the digital forensic investigation of network security management. However, the contemporary state of big data and its challenges with prominence on the digital forensic aspect with a quicker look at the information collected from various stages of the research are studied and then analyzed to model further directions for carrying out an effective digital investigation [11,17]. A fusion-based digital investigation tool motivated by the data fusion model proposed by Joint Director Laboratories (JDL) [7,15,19] has been developed, evaluated [20–22] and experimented in the inspection of various digital crime investigations. Moreover, this chapter is an attempt to explore the possibility of extending the existing digital investigation model to handle voluminous data in network security recognition, discovery and scrutiny. The revision of the existing architecture adopted an inclusion of the look-up table into the same.

7.2 BIG DATA

Big data [9] is described as outsized dimensions of data originated from different mediums such as social media, health care, transport, e-commerce, mobile phones, satellite communications, GPS, media sharing through handheld devices and other modern-day means of communication. Big data is also portrayed by the five V's: variety, velocity, volume, veracity and value [9].

7.2.1 Variety

Big data can originate from a variety of sources such as web pages, network or process logs, posts from social media, emails, documents and data from various sensors [23]. Big data can exist in three different forms, namely, structured, semi-structured and unstructured. Digital forensic investigation of such dissimilar data is complex and hard to achieve [9].

7.2.2 Volume

The Digital Age is dealing with terabytes and petabytes of data; for example, Walmart and Google are dealing with millions of data every day, which ultimately accumulates into petabytes of data per day [1].

7.2.3 Velocity

Velocity of data is growing even in a larger amount day-by-day because as per the statistics by 2020, International Data Corporation has estimated that the types of business transactions will touch 450 billion per day [1,9].

7.2.4 Veracity

The truthfulness and exact dimensions of the data are measured by the fourth V of big data. Per big data, the excellence, ascendancy, metadata administration along with solitude and permissible concerns are also measured by veracity [1,23].

7.2.5 Value

Value refers to the ability to turn the data into a value. The availability of big data can reveal previously unknown insights from data, and this understanding leads to the value [11,15].

7.3 BIG DATA AND DIGITAL FORENSICS

The exponential growth of big data is going to directly affect the digital forensic investigation as the investigation process normally involves a very extensive data set of promising digital evidence to set up the specifics about a digital crime [9,10]. Similar to the other digital investigation, big data digital investigation focuses on reforming all the actions or activities that have happened on a victimized system along with all the supportive data by default recorded by the system, such as registry values, memory residuals, timers, network events, titles of files, date of creation, date of modification, size of files and author of files.

Big data augmented with digital forensics investigation can countenance many confronts, which are as follows [9,10,18]:

A. **Stocking up of petabytes of meaningful data as big data**
Since data sets are enlarged day-by-day to make a digital investigation on this voluminous data, the forensic investigator has to make

storage of this data, which creates a major challenge to the digital forensic community [18].

B. **Rapid indexing of big data**

Indexing structure can make the large and complex data a bit simplified. But when it comes to big data, it becomes a gigantic confront as compared to other data sets to do faster indexing to meet up to the time frame set by the client [9].

C. **Citation methods for big data in the court of law/visualization methods**

Since big data is present in almost all fields of application, an extensive amount of data is required to be present before the court of law. The hefty data always makes it a difficult task for digital investigators to narrate by making it smaller with important key information and prove it before the court of law with justification. So research has to be carried out how to make a suitable presentation of this larger volume of heterogeneous data keeping intact the technical knowledge as well as the interest of digital investigation [10,18,24].

7.4 DIGITAL FORENSIC INVESTIGATION AND ITS ASSOCIATED PROBLEM STATEMENTS

"Digital Forensic Inspection and Investigation is a progression that uses science and technology to examine digital evidence and that develops and tests theories, which can be entered into a court of law, to answer questions about events that occur" [2,6,25]. Digital investigation faces several problems, which are as follows [26]:

- Digital investigations are fetching more time and becoming complex as the dimensions of outsized data requiring investigation continue to breed.

- Digital forensic investigators are experiencing more difficulty to use current forensic tools to trace essential evidence within the enormous volumes of data.

- Logbook files are habitually large in size and multidimensional, which makes the digital investigation and search for supporting evidence more complex.

- Digital evidence [2,6,25] by explanation is the information of probative value stored or transmitted in digital form. It is fragile in nature and can easily be altered or destroyed. It is unique when compared to other forms of documentary evidence.

- Digital forensic investigation tools available are unable to analyze all the data found on the computer system to disclose the overall pattern of the data set, which can help digital investigators decide what steps to take next in their search.

7.5 RELEVANCE OF DATA FUSION APPLICATION IN BIG DATA DIGITAL FORENSICS AND ITS INVESTIGATION

The main purpose of any digital forensics investigation is to collect and prove sufficient valuable digital evidence to allow the criminal perpetrator to be successfully prosecuted. The detection and analysis of cyber threat is a time-consuming activity as a large amount of data is generated from heterogeneous sources and it is needed to be integrated and assimilated to generate a consistent and accurate picture of the underlying phenomena. The major focus in case of investigation of digital crime incidents is in selecting correct patterns, attributes and features and then ranking them so that it can enhance the accuracy of investigation and also can increase the efficiency of the identification, detection and analysis processes.

The key confronts of the digital forensics investigation process are as follows [2,8,11,27]:

- Uncovering, diagnosing and segregating the volume of data;

- Safeguarding data subject to discovery;

- Recapturing embedded files;

- Carrying out on-site inspections;

- Bonding of expert assistance.

To deal with these challenges, traditional digital forensic models and tools have to be well equipped with a variety of application techniques to become aware of and shield against digital crimes. Data fusion and decision mining along with visualization techniques and machine learning techniques [16,19] can diminish the intricacy that stays alive within the data.

To develop a digital forensic investigation model to deal with big data requires a suitable method for selecting architecture and adopting alternative techniques for cost-effective system requirements [18]. The requirements and guidelines of digital forensic and its investigation involving big data should advocate an archetype in which the blueprint and growth flow from overall investigational requirements and constraints to a specification involving applications of data fusion, decision mining and machine learning techniques to knob the confronts of big data and its investigations. To build a digital investigation model involving big data, various factors should be taken into consideration [9,18], which are as follows:

- Digital forensic investigation model involving big data should stick to the steps of digital investigation as well as guidelines for digital forensics.

- Computational science techniques should be able to inspect and optimize the investigation process of various computer frauds and cybercrime cases.

- A forensic investigator should be able to extract the maximum digital evidence information keeping in mind that inspection will include 5 V's of big data.

- Optimization of the data analysis process should be done by adhering to the data collection process.

- Optimization and accuracy in the digital investigation process should be achieved irrespective of the data being analyzed.

7.6 DATA FUSION

Data fusion involves the application of sensory information from various numbers of sensors so that information in a large quantity can be collected from the environment under inspection [7,15]. Data fusion is also a natural process that happens in every human being and animal. Humans have five sense organs, using which they collect the information about a particular situation and environment and finally draw a concluding remark on it. Data fusion theory described by Wald [15,19] is a ceremonial structure in which data originating from different sources are aligned and framed to a common format. The main purpose of data fusion is to derive information of superior quality. The exact quality of the information is dependent on the application or case being solved. Data fusion systems are developed to draw qualitative information rather than concluding decisions. The decision-making process can be augmented with such type of systems. The data fusion system automation first became functional from the late 1970s by military systems. A plenty of research was being carried out about data fusion all through the 1980s. A data fusion subpanel was established by the U.S. Department of Defense (DoD) in 1986, which is also the sub-panel of the JDL commonly referred to as Technical Panel for C3.

The data fusion systems in the military world were functional during the late 1980s and were rapidly developed from that time. They were first applied in the military domain, but later on, the theory of fusion is also applied in the civilian domain. The theory of fusion is famous in ocean surveillance, air-to-air defense, surface-to-air defense, battlefield intelligence, surveillance and target acquisition, and strategic warning and defense. In all of the application areas, the main focus was on the locality, classification and recognition of entities. Residential applications include the accomplishment of robotics, automated control of industrial manufacturing systems, growth of smart buildings and healthcare applications [19]. The theory of data fusion is also now extended towards the area of data, information and network security.

7.6.1 The JDL Practical Data Fusion Procedural Model

With the hard work and endeavor, JDL/DFS data fusion procedural model was developed that explains an elevated practical view of the theory of data fusion and its levels as well as functions at each level. The JDL functional data fusion procedural model (Figure 7.1) has the following eight constituents [7,15,19]:

- **Sources:** User inputs are collected and fed to the data fusion system through sources. The most probable sources are local sensors, distributed sensors, human input and a priori information from databases.

- **Preprocessing:** This component is also known as "Level 0 Processing" or "Process Refinement". Preprocessing step of data fusion system involves initial processing to allocate the data to the next levels of processing. This step of data fusion system concentrates on data that is appropriate to the present situation, thereby diminishing the consignment of the fusion system.

- **Low-level fusion or level 1 processing:** This step of fusion is also known as object enhancement. The main focus of this step is to fuse

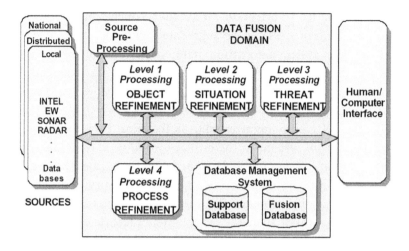

FIGURE 7.1   JDL functional data fusion process model [7,15].

the sensor information to attain a distill representation of an individual entity. This step is responsible for fulfilling the following four functionalities:

- **Coalition and alignment of data:** It involves the positioning of data collected from various sensors to a universal orientation format.

- **Alliance of data:** It involves combination, sorting or correlating the events being observed from multiple sensors so that they can end up with a single entity.

- **Trailing and tracking of data:** It involves the amalgamation of numerous surveillances of inspected data to approximate the place, location and swiftness of an entity.

- **Recognition of data:** It merges data related to distinctiveness to filter the inferences of an object's uniqueness or categorization.

Level 1 low-level fusion profits from the use of diversified sensors and the service of spatially dispersed sensors as well as the submission of nonsensor providing information.

- **Level 2 processing:** This step is also known as situation refinement. It expands a background explanation of relations between entities. It concentrates on relational information to narrate the connotation of a group of entities. It focuses on aggregating the entities and event, interpreting the event activities and lastly interpreting the context. As a result of this step, antagonistic deeds and patterns are indicated. It successfully enlarges and improves the absoluteness, steadiness and abstraction levels of the current situation portrayal shaped by object alteration.

- **Level 3 processing:** This step is also known as a threat and hazard refinement. It explores the current situation and forecasts it into the future to derive presumptions about promising upshots. It recognizes the impending opponent's intent, lethality and the respective vulnerabilities.

- **Level 4 processing:** This level of fusion procedure is also known as procedural refinement. It is also mentioned as a metaprocess with an objective to optimize the overall presentation of the fusion procedural system. It again involves four subfunctions.

  - Presentation valuation deals with live and real time-based presentation and long-term presentation valuations.

  - Method control functionality deals with the improvement of multiple-level fusion and its information retrieval.

  - Foundational origin retrieval and requirements finding identify the foundation-specific requirements to gather valid and relevant information.

  - Mission management deals with managing the foundational origins to obtain mission objectives and goals. Mission management may not be involved in the main task of sphere of specific data fusion functions. This kind of subfunction is normally kept outside the data fusion procedures shown in Figure 7.1.

- **The database management system:** It is responsible for storage and retrieval from several data fusion-based databases. Its main functionalities may include data repossession, storage space determination, archiving, firmness, queries regarding relational databases and protection and security of data.

- **The human–computer interface data fusion system:** It allows the users to provide input to the fusion levels for further processing. The output of the data fusion process is also communicated back to the user by allowing human input into the data fusion process.

7.7 REVISED DATA FUSION-BASED DIGITAL INVESTIGATION MODEL FOR DIGITAL FORENSIC AND NETWORK THREAT MANAGEMENT

Many digital forensic exploration models and practices are available, which are currently used in solving computer frauds and cybercrime cases to retrieve potential legal digital evidence. But with the theatrical exponential intensification of the digital technology, computer frauds and cybercrime are increasingly progressing too. Thus, it has raised a requirement of inflating the research work in the field of digital forensics and its investigation. So an inclusive, interrelated and comprehensive amalgamation of information and facts approaching from a variety of heterogeneous origins along with sensible and precise uncovering and examination is the call of the hour. Hence, this chapter modifies the previous work by stressing the formalization, speedy and consistent detection and appropriate as well as precise analysis of potential valuable digital evidence from diversified sources simultaneously.

A fusion-based digital exploration model is already developed [20–22,28] based on JDL [7,15,19], which has been experimented in solving computer frauds and cybercrime cases. In this chapter, the research study is done to extend the fusion-based digital exploration model to handle outsized data such as big data for network threat identification, detection and examination for better timely and accurate results. The modification of the existing fusion-based digital investigation model approved the inclusion of the look-up table into the already-developed structural design for network security management and threat analysis.

This chapter modifies the on-hand fusion-based investigation tool (Figure 7.2) by regrouping and remerging the steps of digital investigational activities and augmenting the look-up table, which can act as an associative memory and can maintain a one-to-one correspondence with the steps of digital forensic inspection and examination of crime cases. The regrouping and remerging in the revised fusion-based digital investigation model will maintain an equilibrium between the steps of data fusion and their outputs with the investigation steps and also can deliver more quality data for further exploration with an intent to retrieve digital evidence. The model also supports postmortem forensic analysis by preserving the necessary potential legal digital evidence. With big data everywhere, the theory of data fusion can provide security intelligence by shortening the time of correlating outsized, voluminous, heterogeneous sources for forensic purposes [18,23,27].

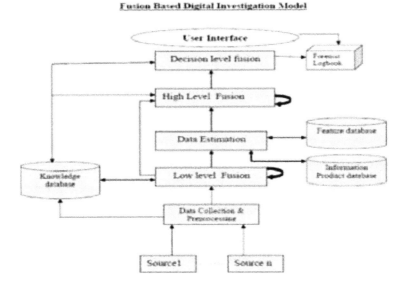

FIGURE 7.2   Fusion-based digital investigation model. (Adapted Satpathy et al. [20,21].)

As described previously, data fusion is a theory to blend or amalgamate the raw facts, figures and information leading to outsized data called big data from a variety of sources so that the fusion process can fabricate a precise and elevated eminence of information [19,14,29]. The intention of data fusion is data cleanup (getting rid of irrelevant information) and data renovation (i.e., translation of raw data into meaningful information of value) and to engender data machinery (where big data can be conked out into slighter components for enhanced scrutiny) [18].

The revised fusion-based digital investigation model for handling outsized data termed as big data for timely and accurate examination and detection of crime scenes is shown in Figure 7.3. The activities of the revised model at different levels of fusion can be grouped into the following steps. Each and every step is further narrated briefly with its equilibrium being maintained with the steps of digital forensic investigation.

- Preprocessing,

- Dispensation of criminal activities in various levels of fusion,

- Pronouncement about the digital crime activities and making it traceable to the origin,

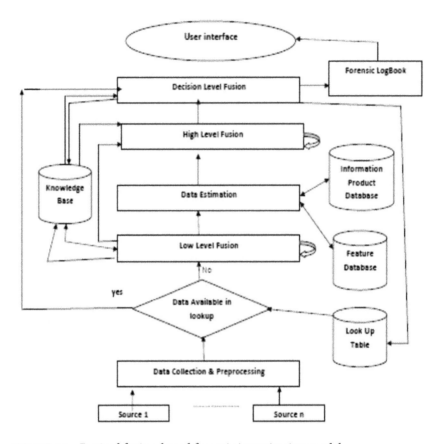

FIGURE 7.3   Revised fusion-based forensic investigation model.

- Digital evidence accretion,

- Data renovation by converting the raw facts and figures into meaningful information as digital evidence,

- Data diminution (diminishing the big data set into a smaller size to make the digital inspection more sensible and reasonable).

The phases of the revised fusion-based digital investigation model can be described as follows.

Source: The sources for digital forensic investigation of any computer frauds and cybercrime are all possible heterogeneous diversified sources that have been acknowledged after a digital crime is reported and handed over to the forensic investigative agencies to find the root cause and also the cybercriminal committed the crime.

7.7.1 Data Collection and Preprocessing

The primary step of examination and inspection in the fusion-based investigation model is to collect and assimilate data and process it so that data being collected can be semantically understandable attributes of entities [20,22]. The information and facts gathered about the event can then be aligned in moment in time, space or dimension units. The retrieved output information is required to be saved to the knowledge database.

7.7.2 Look-Up Table

This acts as a storage container of recently accessed useful patterns of interest related to the digital crime cases. Such storage is helpful in maintaining the timely detection and analysis of the simplified criminal events, which do require complex investigational steps or procedures. With the help of the look-up table, one can bypass the other upper levels of fusion processing and can directly access the forensic logbook for documentation.

7.7.3 Low-Level Fusion

This level of fusion activity mainly focuses on data cleanup, data alteration and data diminution [20]. This level of fusion in a digital investigation model lowers the load of big data by its volume and variety by concomitantly hanging on to meaningful information and thereby advances its eminence, with a minimum loss of detail.

It is mainly concerned with data, which are as follows [15,19]:

- Data cleanup (eradicates immaterial information),

- Data alteration (translates the unprocessed data into prearranged information),

- Data diminution (trimming down the outsized data set into a lesser volume to make the examination more practical and feasible).

So the above points facilitate the fusion activities to eradicate less important data from the larger volume of big data depending on the specific digital crime case being examined. This level of processing will be helpful to narrow down the search space into a case specific so that it can be easier to manage ending with saving of valuable time in digital forensic examination and inspection.

7.7.4 Data Estimation Phase

This phase takes into account the behavioral model of the system, which is studied from data stored in the feature database and the knowledge acquired by the knowledge base. Based on the estimation of the behavioral model, the current event data is estimated. The essential attributes from the ordered data sets and the fusion-based investigation system save them to an information product database for future examination and analysis.

7.7.5 High-Level Fusion

In this step of the digital investigation model, the entities or events are bonded with a relationship being studied from their surroundings portrayal. The establishment of such a relationship includes analyzing and interpreting the criminal activities as well as crime events and ends with relative elucidation. The high-level fusion processing may include pattern identification, detection and analysis with the help of clustering, classification, association and mining [16,19]. The concluding remarks of such results obtained would be indicative of disparaging performance blueprints. These features form a feature space fused to identify and classify them to serve for attack detection and recognition. It effectively extends and enhances the completeness, consistency and level of abstraction of the situation description.

7.7.6 Decision-Level Fusion

The useful blueprints obtained from this level of fusion processing require further attention of inspection to derive justification and relevancy of the identified patterns from it. Moreover, to conclude with the significant patterns further, it explores the present state of affairs, circumstances and schemes in the future to sketch inferences about achievable upshots. This level of fusion processing focuses on finding out intention, lethality and prospects [17,30,31]. The examined and well-proved patterns of interest capable of tracing the computer frauds and cybercrime into its origin are documented in the forensic logbook. This logbook acts as an evidence of support for the digital forensic investigator, who can use it as an evidentiary report generation storehouse to be used as connoisseur witness in the court of law [8,12].

7.7.7 Forensic Logbook

The forensic logbook is an evidential record-keeping system. The word "forensics" refers to the postmortem examination of virtual digital evidence [6,8,12,25]. The digital information in the virtual world of zeros and ones is incarcerated and stored in the forensic logbook in a prearranged format to keep track of date of occurrence of event and time of occurrence of the event, prowler's IP address and target event's IP address, users, type of criminal event, and victory or collapse of the criminal activity, source of request for recognition/confirmation, entity's information, its brief introduction, and if it has been deleted, then time of deletion, etc. The time tag is also recorded for criminal activity. Documentary report is a continuous process starting from data collection and preprocessing to decision-level fusion processing. It can be used as strong digital evidence of support as expert testimony in the court of law.

7.7.8 User Interface

The user interface is a medium of the communication interface between the digital forensic investigator and the forensic logbook. The supervisor and digital forensic experts can correspond with the forensic logbook through it. The accuracy of the investigation can be enhanced with an external source of knowledge as supplementary information, and thus, it can be saved to the knowledge base, making the fusion processing more dynamic.

Further, the output of fusion-based investigation model is grouped and integrated to establish a mapping (Table 7.1) between the phases of digital investigation and domains of data fusion theory. The grouping of activities maintains an equilibrium between the steps of the digital investigation process and domains of data fusion to handle the outsized data called big data to produce more quality data for final decision analysis.

7.8 PRACTICABILITY AND LIKELIHOOD OF DIGITAL INVESTIGATION MODEL

The revised fusion-based digital investigation model can be used as an evidence acquiring medium for retrieving Offline Admissible Legal Digital Evidence for digital forensic investigating agencies, including conservation and permanence of evidence, and intelligibility of the digital investigation methods. As the acceptability and heaviness are the two necessary attributes in the permissible suitability of digital evidence [1,11], the court of law has to tackle with concerns relating to the disparity between the narrative scientific evidence and the legal evidence.

The main objective of the fusion-based digital investigation model is to gather the evidentiary information and data that can be demonstrated to the people to prove that the digital crime is committed even after it is over. Along with that, timely identification and detection of the criminal activities, as well as accuracy of investigative results, are the important things to

TABLE 7.1   Mapping Phases of Digital Investigation Model into Fusion-Based Investigation Tool

Data Fusion Levels	Digital Investigation Phase	Mapping Activities as an Output from Fusion-Based Digital Investigation Model
Source	Training and preparing the team	Consciousness, agreement, sketch, announcement, corroboration
Data collection and preprocessing	Collection and preservation	Digital media, devices, imperative events, non-imperative events, abolition procedure
Look-up table	Timely/accurate detection	Quick access and reference
Low-level fusion	Investigation/ examination/ analysis	Crime categories, alignment format, alignment rules
Data estimation		System model
High-level fusion	Investigation/ examination/ analysis	Establishment of relationships between crime events, reformation of the event scene, event construal appropriate elucidation indication of disparaging manners of interesting patterns. Comprehensiveness, uniformity, generalization of the situation and its fine-tuning
Decision-level fusion	Investigation/ examination/ analysis	log files, file, events log, data, information evidence, evidence report
User interface and forensic logbook	Presentation in the court of law	Evidence clarification, evidence predisposed, new-fangled policies, up-to-the-minute procedures and steps in the investigation
Databases	Future reference history	Digital crime taxonomy, cybercriminal profiles, their intention, lethality

be considered to be receptive to the needs of the law enforcement agencies and protective of the chain of evidence of digital intrusions.

7.9 CONCLUSION AND FUTURE WORK

The existence of big data in digital forensic examination and investigation of various types of computer frauds and cyber crime can make the investigation process crucial because of the association of various factors like dimensions, diversification and multifaceted interdependence among the data to be investigated. But the conventional methods for the digital forensic investigation adopt one or more existing forensic tools to examine each data resource. But when voluminous, heterogeneous data is involved in one digital crime event, it is difficult to aggregate, correlate the events into a common reference format and hence will end up with inaccurate findings as well as the inefficiency of the investigation process. This chapter has revised a novel fusion-based digital investigational framework for the digital forensic investigation that includes assorted big data. The revised digital investigational model mainly focuses upon volume, variety of data as well as timeliness, consistency and accuracy of the data. Future work of our study relies on the design of detection algorithms and machine intelligence techniques to grip various types of network threats involving big data, and digital technological platform stays useful for well-beings.

REFERENCES

1. N. Beebe and J. Clark, Dealing with terabyte data sets in digital investigations. In: *Advances in Digital Forensics*, Springer, 3–16, 2005.
2. C. Shields, O. Frieder, and M. Maloof. A system for the proactive, continuous, and efficient collection of digital forensic evidence, *Journal of Digital Investigation*, 8, S3–S13, 2011. doi: 10.1016/j.diin.2011.05.002.
3. Digital Forensic Research Workshop (DFRWS) Research Road Map, 2001, Utica, NY.
4. Access Data Corporation, www.accessdata.com, 2005.
5. Guidance Software, Inc., www.guidancesoftware.com, 2005.
6. E. Casey, *Digital Evidence and Computer Crime: Forensic Science, Computer and the Internet*, Academic Press, Cambridge, MA, 2011.
7. F. Castanedo, A review of data fusion techniques, *The Scientific World Journal*, 2013, 19, 2013, Hindawi Publishing Corporation.
8. E. Casey (ed.), *Handbook of Computer Crime Investigation*, Academic Press, Cambridge, MA, 2001.
9. S. Sagiroglu and D. Sinanc, Big data: A review, *In International Conference on Collaboration Technologies and Systems (CTS)*, Philadelphia, PA, IEEE, pp. 42–47, 2013.
10. S. Zawoad and R. Hasan, Digital Forensics in the Age of Big Data: Challenges, Approaches, and Opportunities, *ResearchGate*, 2015. doi: 10.1109/hpcc-css-icess.
11. D. Brezinski and T. Killalea, Guidelines for Evidence Collection and Archiving, RFC3227, February 2002.
12. O. S. Kerr, *Computer Crime Law*, 2nd edn, West (Thomson R), Toronto, 2009.
13. SAS, Big Data Meets Big Data Analytics, Technical Report. www.sas.com/resources/whitepaper/wp46345.pdf.
14. M. Damshenas, A. Dehghantanha, and R. Mahmoud, A survey on digital forensics trends, *International Journal of Cyber-Security and Digital Forensics (IJCSDF)*, 3(4), 209–234, 2014.
15. D. L. Hall and J. Llinas, An introduction to multi-sensor data fusion, *In Proceedings of the IEEE*, 85(1), 6–23, 1997.

16. J. Han and M. Kamber, *Data Mining: Concepts and Techniques*, 2nd edn, San Francisco, CA, Elsevier, 2005.
17. M. Ponec, P. Giura, H. Bronnimann, and J. Wein, Highly efficient techniques for N/w forensics, *In CCS07: 14th ACM Conference on Computer and Communications Security*, Alexandria, VA, pp. 150–160, October 2007.
18. AICPA, Big Data Listed as Top Issue Facing Forensic and Valuation Professionals in Next Two to Five Years: AICPA Survey, http://goo.gl/1BgdWB, 2014.
19. J. Bleiholder and F. Naumann, Data fusion, *ACM Computing Surveys*, 41(1), 1–41, 2008.
20. S. Satpathy and A. Mohapatra, A data fusion based digital investigation model as an effective forensic tool in the risk assessment and management of cyber security systems, *In 7th International Conference on Computing, Communication and Control technologies (CCCT)*, Orlando, FL, 2009.
21. S. Satpathy, S. K. Pradhan, and B. N. B. Ray, A digital investigation tool based on data fusion in management of cyber security systems, *International Journal of IT and Knowledge Management*, 3(2), 561–565, 2010.
22. S. Satpathy, S. K. Pradhan, and B.N. B. Ray, Rule based decision mining with JDL data fusion model for computer forensics: A hypothetical case study, *International Journal of Computer Science and Information Security*, 9(12), 93–100, 2011. http://sites.google.com/site/ijcsis.
23. A. A. Cárdenas, P. K. Manadhata, and S. P. Rajan, Big Data Analytics for Security, University of Texas at Dallas, HP Labs, Fujitsu Laboratories of America.
24. B. Davis, How Much Data We Create Daily, http://goo.gl/a0ImFT, 2013.
25. E. Casey, N/w traffic as a source of evidence: Tool strengths, weaknesses, and future needs, *Digital Investigation*, 1(1), 28–43, 2004.
26. S. Garfinkel, Digital forensics research: The next 10 years, *In Proceeding of DFRWS Annual Forensics Research Conference*, Portland, OR, August 2010.
27. D. Das, U. Shaw, and S. P. Medhi, Realizing digital forensics as a big data challenge, *Fourth International Conference on "Computing for Sustainable Global Development"*, New Delhi, India, 01–03 March, 2017.
28. H. Fatima, S. Satpathy, S. Mahapatra, G. N. Dash, and S. K. Pradhan, Data fusion & visualization application for network forensic investigation: A Case study, *IEEE 2nd International Conference on Anti Cyber Crimes*, Abha, Saudi Arabia, , King Khalid University, March 26–27, 2017.
29. R. Pochampally, A. D. Sarma, X. L. Dong, A. Meliou, and D. Srivastava, Fusing data with correlations, *In Sigmod*, 2014.
30. M. Liberatore, R. Erdely, T. Kerle, B. N. Levine, and C. Shields, Forensic investigation of peer-to-peer file sharing networks, *In Proceeding of DFRWS Annual Digital Forensics Research Conference*, Portland, OR, August 2010.
31. Z. T. Fernando, I. S. Thaseen, and Ch. Aswani Kumar, Network attacks identification using consistency based feature selection and self-organizing maps, *2014 IEEE Conference on N/ws and Soft Computing*, Guntur, Andhra Pradesh.

CHAPTER 8

Phishing Prevention Guidelines

Shweta Shankhwar, Dhirendra Pandey,
and Raees Ahmad Khan

Babasaheb Bhimrao Ambedkar University (Central University)

CONTENTS

8.1 PHISHING

Over the last decade, phishing attacks have grown considerably on the Internet. Phishing is the process of enticing people into visiting fraudulent websites and persuading them to enter their personal information. Numbers of a phishing email are spread with the aim of making web users believe that they are communicating with a trusted entity [1]. Phishing is deployed by using advanced technical means. Phishing refers to sending of spurious emails that are usually forged by the phishers to lure a user in their snares, leading the user to lose his/her sensitive data or credential, identity theft, pecuniary loss, etc.

8.1.1 Why Phishing Works

Ever since the cyber threat, namely, phishing, has come into existence, numerous hazards and hassles have encroached loud and mis-happenings have gone by leaps and bounds. The most perilous of these phishing attacks which have boomed out in the present era is email phishing executed via obfuscated URL/malicious URL [2]. There are naive users in ample who cannot make out the difference between the authentic and crafted emails. Hence in a jiffy, the phisher can put a snare to execute his slyness. The toddling users for whom e-communication is a greenhorn paradise are very much unaware and ignorant of threats over the same [3]. Their indifference and unawareness are the main flaws that let the phishers lurk into their private ambience and impale or breach security without their acknowledgment [4].

8.1.2 Phishing in Enterprise

Phishers launch a mass attack to hook naive users or many times, to a targeted user of an enterprise without his knowledge. Scrutinizing the activities and behaviors of the relevant user, the phisher tries to attack the user in a friendly or a coaxing manner [5]. The research and the keen analysis done by the phisher are subjected to the user being how much social and gregarious in digital space. Phishers utilize this vulnerability of humane factor to the fullest for transforming his malicious theories into catastrophic outcomes [6]. The attacks of social engineering comprise psychological manipulation, bluffing and fooling to gain the confidential or sensitive information. It also includes communications referring to emails and others that instigate a sense of anxiety, urgency or likewise in the heart and soul of the victim [7,8].

All of the above are used as mass email phishing attacks and also to target specific persons in enterprise environs with a motive of acquiring sensitive information. This is not initiated by any random fraudster but is likely to be planned and executed by an acquaintance as an insider threat. The main susceptibility exploited by phishers is familiarity exploit, which is done through social engineering [9]. The users' human nature itself acts as a psychological and behavioral agent; further, it is axiomatically rational one. As observed in all the phishing attacks, the phisher specifically executes his plantings through the means of obfuscated URLs and snares up the user to fall victim.

8.2 PHISHING PREVENTION GUIDELINES

Phishing prevention guidelines are proposed to avoid the phishing caused by social facets (social human factor). Social facets or human errors are the factors that could be prevented by users only [10]. User or enterprise employee should be aware as well as alert not to fall prey in phishing attack [11]. To make them aware and alert towards phishing and other cybercrime, some guidelines are proposed, which are explained in the following sections.

8.2.1 Cyber Awareness and Hygiene

The potential online threats as in email phishing have proved out to be a big blow to the confidence trust reputation and pecuniary facets of users in prevalence [12]. In order to meet the metaphysical challenges, the precautionary measures ought to be implicit in the actions of users [13]. Setting clear guidelines for Internet and email usage as well as securing one's online presence in every arena of cyberspace is the soul motto of cyber awareness and hygiene.

E-communication or social media is the mode of prime concern and attention. If the user does not select the right settings on our social media accounts, then photos and videos posted by us can be viewed, downloaded and then used by others without our knowledge, and on a greater note, these indifferences towards the security measures can even lead to a potential phishing attack. In order to do away with these maligns, the right privacy settings and content sharing filters on social media should be selected, so that the information, photos and videos can be shared only with the trusted ones or acquaintances.

Refraining from the clutches of phishing is defined by spreading of awareness and educating the people of ill-aftermath of this attack simultaneously providing people the general information on phishing and the related activities. It is very important to educate the people and spread awareness because the coming days are going to be full of e-communication and e-commerce. Imparting awareness will include presenting papers and delivering lectures to a large number of masses on phishing-related hassles and setting up regular reminders to the customers and prospects about the details of the services they are employed in.

8.2.2 Phishing Prevention on Ground Level

Phishing prevention on ground level defines the basic but relevant guidelines that will guide the naive user to safely use the Internet, which are as follows:

1. Always be vigilant about the latest technologies through which phishing could occur, stay updated with the latest technologies, target to shut down the phishing websites and continue to monitor which are the leading websites used by the people and how they are functioning. Always be secured with home computing, making of a tight security arrangement on the personal system through which the transactions are made and further, keeping the operating system up to date and installation of antivirus to stay healthy rather than being a phishing victim.

2. If a pop-up message bottles up while using the Internet, never click on any button present on the pop-up (not even close button), as they might contain malware.

3. Never click on suspicious links or attachments; that is, never click on links or files received in email, text message or social media from an unfamiliar source as it may be an attempt to infect the computer system with malware.

4. Apply the secured browser settings; that is, always choose an updated version of the browser and install safe browsing tools to protect from phishers, hackers and malware.

5. In case of being cyberstalked, end the communication with the stalker immediately; "report and block" the stalker for the best precautionary measure so as to refrain oneself from being bullied or harassed.

6. Limitation/prohibition of sharing potential identification information or any family details, such as name, date of birth, mobile number (registered in the bank), marriage date, PAN number, passport number and Aadhaar card details, over social media sites, matrimonial sites, e-wallets and others.

7. Do rigorous updation of software, and never install software, games, music and apps from unknown sources as the phishers usually target software vulnerabilities and gain access to private

information of users and putting them at risk, so it gets mandatory to have updated all the relevant software with latest and finest security measures.

8.2.3 Phishing Precautionary Measures at Enterprise Environs

As far as the enterprise environs are concerned, most of the phishing attacks prevail in the related arena; the preventions along with defensive lines may be in identifying between genuine and imposter accounts. Most of the phishers use the tantrums, for instance, imposter accounts, spoofed emails, usage fake URLs/links to click with persuasion techniques, etc. One of the striking and remarkable points about a phishing attack in enterprise environs is that usually, the phishers attack a victim using a potential vulnerability. Basically, the employees overlook vulnerability, and their negligence and behavior response make them fall prey in a phishing attack.

As per the gist acquired through the study and development of anti-PhiEE model, the insider threat and the phishing attacks from the familiar sources, common acquaintance and activities are the ones that have been mostly responsible for the launch of phishing attacks in an enterprise. Therefore, for the autonomous preventions to this deterring miserability of enterprise employees as emulating typical phishers' actions, the emails are usually aimed to lure employees in a manner of inflicting and manipulating through visceral factor and familiarity cues, etc., thereby provoking them to click obfuscated links. Each phishing email contains sex essential clues that would help employees or users to identify and do away with setbacks as guided underneath:

1. Check if there are mismatched name and address in the From field in the email.

2. Check if there are errors such as misspelling, incorrect grammar and odd spacing.

3. Make persuasion and need encouragement to take immediate action, sense of urgency, sympathy, etc.

4. Check if there is a mismatch between the link text and the link address displayed when hovering the mouse over it.

5. Again, this email looks reasonable enough though it's lacking a specific detail – no customer name or account number is mentioned.

Finally, the email is signed but the name isn't identifiable and therefore not verifiable.

6. At last, alert and intuition, that is, the overall feeling that something is not right (e.g., users were not expecting it).

8.2.4 Sturdy and Meticulous Web Development Is Recommended

Always, while designing, a website developer should keep in mind how and when a phisher can get into action. Keeping all the best things possible to stop phishing, they should design a website with the latest technology possible. They should be able to evaluate at which instances a website can be attacked by the phishers, should keenly observe the website, and if anything persists, let the IP address fall and make the necessary changes to maintain the credibility of the website. They should follow all the procedures and policies of creating and functioning of a website, and try to make the website as safe as possible. All attributes of software security (such as confidentiality, integrity and availability [CIA]) should be included in the software requirement elicitation process and also at each phase of the software development life cycle.

8.2.5 Suggestive Measures for other Cybercrime

The ATM (automated teller machine) electronic transaction is playing a very persistent and pervasive role. The authentication and authorization are conventional methods based on possession of debit card details and security number (personal identification number [PIN]), which are not reliable, as skimmers, keypad overlay, shoulder suffering and hidden cameras are used to commit fraud. Security against these kinds of advanced persistent threats or fraud is not sufficient to deal. Therefore, a secure layer of authentication, that is, a one-time password (OTP) approach for protection from advanced persistent threats or fraud, is developed. It is needed to include OTP to reduce fraud and its impact. It is a unique thought process about secure electronic transaction of ATM security, and builds trust and confidence of users towards Alternate Delivery Banking Channels. ATM/EDC Digital Swapping Keypad and ATM/EDC Censored Keypad Shield Cover for the delicate level of trust and confidence towards electronic transaction ATM are also recommended [14].

Nowadays, Internet anonymity is a serious problem. Therefore, the Proactive Cyber Anonymity Minimization Model (PCAMM) [15] is developed, which will be an inclusive guide and assistance towards cybercrime investigators. This developed approach is based on geolocation-based authentication through an IP address. This approach enhances safety through secured access to Internet services with accurate geolocation tracking. The cybercriminals will be alert and afraid to erode their anonymity and chances of getting caught will increase as their original geolocation could be disclosed through this idea. This proposed model could drastically decrease the cybercrime rate as it is a deterrent, security-enhancing cyber investigation process. It is a time-saving, accurate process with less effort; it will help in monitoring the behavior of the user and can avoid cyber frauds at a larger scale.

8.3 IMPLEMENTATION OF PHISHING PREVENTION GUIDELINES

The proposed phishing prevention guidelines are implemented in the real-case scenarios as of phishing attack. To implement and validate the proposed guidelines, some weight for each guideline is assumed according to their impact. Through these guidelines, assigning weight for the prevention of phishing attack is done in different scenarios. The weight for each guideline is given in Table 8.1. Prevention of phishing attack is based on the following range: worst = 0–0.5, average = 0.6–1.4 and high = above 1.4.

Therefore, four case studies are discussed in detail for implementation and validation, which are as follows:

Case study 1: An imposter of the legitimate domain of an enterprise was registered; here, the enterprise's employees were the target. The name of the enterprise was used by phishers via the bogus domain to send spoofed emails to the employees. The striking point here is that all the emails were sent to employees in the name of the CEO of the enterprise. The email contained the name(s) of targeted individuals of work environs. This makes it so implicit that phishers have thoroughly done their homework, that is, social engineering about the enterprise and its employees. Invoking a sense of urgency, the reply

TABLE 8.1 Phishing Prevention Guideline Weight

SN.	Phishing Prevention Guidelines	Weight
1	The cyber awareness and hygiene	0.4
2	Phishing prevention on ground level	0.6
3	Phishing precautionary measures at enterprise environs	0.8
4	Sturdy and meticulous web	0.2

or reversion of the employees would eventually tend the employee to lose their professional and personal information. A number of high-risk targets such as an elite member of the financial team or persons with access to confidential were usually targeted by phishers in the enterprise environs.

Case study 2: Mr. Malhotra – an initial entrepreneur, then a successful businessperson – not always proved himself to be financially acumen. Unluckily, he was not aware/immuned from falling a victim to a phishing scam that inflicts him immense stress and could have led him to absolute insolvency. This was the case when Mr. Malhotra received an email with a URL/link. It was a bank where he has a bank account asking or informing him that there has been familiar activity observed on his bank account, is that you? The email also asked that Mr. Malhotra not confirmed his details, and his card may be suspended soon.

The email seemed to be perfectly authentic as there were a bank logo and details. He had been using his debit card quite frequently so it sounded genuine to him that the bank people were following up for security reasons. Mr. Malhotra was unable to differentiate between legitimate and phishing. Mr. Malhotra at a point got skeptical of the email when it asked him to enter his personal credential as he had once received an email bi his bank that said, "No legitimate bank" would ever ask one to enter one's personal details. But at that point of time, Mr. Malhotra was so curious to just get his account sorted and he really didn't ponder and proceeded. Thus, a sense of fear and urgency was forced upon him, which made him feel this to be so urgent to act promptly. Mr. Malhotra clicked on the link that redirected him to an illegitimate website that seemed to be quite genuine and further entered his bank details. He thought this was the end of the problem but who knew it was just the beginning of his misery. After a couple of days, when Mr. Malhotra checked his bank statement, he was shocked that an amount Rs 1,000,000 was withdrawn from his account. He notified the bank, and then he came to know that he has fallen prey of an email phishing attack.

Case study 3: One of our acquaintances was targeted to a phishing attack by the means of a bogus customer satisfaction survey. The individuals that were target had been lured of getting a sure shot gift or reward amount for filling up the survey form. Although they were never supposed to get a single penny, they finally asked to put into their credit/debit card details which they did not mind to provide. Very soon, they got to know that their card details are stolen and phishers had used these details to launch the phishing attack.

Case study 4: A trendy attack by phishers is when they craft a replica of the website or forge the website a genuine organization. In 2014, a lady precisely a research assistant received an email sent by her friend. She read the email and found it relevant to her work. The email was pointing to a conference to hold soon and the lady found that the conference is related to her domain. To gain more knowledge, she clicked on the link present in the same email and redirected it to the conference website. She had a glance of conference specification, registration and call for paper and publications details. She immediately decided to participate in the conference as an author to publish the research manuscript, as it was a nice opportunity. She submitted her research manuscript for publication and did registration for the conference with Rs 25,000 through the website. Thereafter, for the successful manuscript submission and completion of the registration process, she waited for a few weeks to get the response for further process. It was a tense situation when she didn't receive any response email. There was no trail of website and the link related to it where she submitted and registered for the manuscript publication. She lost her cool and immediately lodged the complaint for the same with a sign of losing a huge amount as well as the essential manuscript. Later on, it was found to be an email phishing case [15].

8.4 VALIDATION OF PHISHING PREVENTION GUIDELINES

All possible states or scenarios of the above-discussed case studies are listed in this section. The prevention of phishing attack is calculated through proposed phishing prevention guidelines. Phishing prevention guidelines have some weight and the range: worst = 0, average = 0.8–1.4 and high = 2.0, as discussed in the above section and listed in Table 8.1. It is observed that the state-1 has not followed any guidelines as the prevention of phishing attack weight is 0. The state-12 gains the highest weight of 2.0 as it followed all the proposed guidelines. The strength of the prevention of phishing attack can be easily observed with their achieved weight in different states of case studies as is mentioned in Table 8.2.

TABLE 8.2   Validation of Phishing Prevention Guidelines

All Possible Scenarios of Case Study	Cyber Awareness and Hygiene	Phishing Prevention on Ground Level	Phishing Precautionary Measures at Enterprise Environs	Sturdy and Meticulous Web Development	Prevention of Phishing Attack
Scenario 1	0	0	0	0	0
Scenario 2	0	0.6	0	0	0.6
Scenario 3	0	0	0.8	0	0.8
Scenario 4	0	0.6	0.8	0	1.4
Scenario 5	0	0	0	0	0
Scenario 6	0	0.6	0	0	0.6
Scenario 7	0	0	0.8	0	0.8
Scenario 8	0	0.6	0.8	0	1.4
Scenario 9	0.4	0	0	0.2	0.6
Scenario 10	0.4	0.6	0	0.2	1.2
Scenario 11	0.4	0	0.8	0.2	1.4
Scenario 12	0.4	0.6	0.8	0.2	2.0
Scenario 13	0.4	0	0	0.2	0.6
Scenario 14	0.4	0.6	0	0.2	1.2
Scenario 15	0.4	0	0.8	0.2	1.4
Scenario 16	0.4	0.6	0.8	0.2	2

8.5 SUMMARY

The phishing prevention guidelines for enterprise employees or naive users are proposed. These guidelines will help and train enterprise employees and online users to recognize fake or phishing websites and also make them aware and alert from cybercrimes. Some suggestive measures against other cybercrime are also discussed for the prevention and protection of naive user's cybersafety. It would keep them secured in cyber, social and monitory aspects, and also, it would help them spread cyber awareness through mouth publicity.

REFERENCES

1. Tankard, Colin, Advanced persistent threats and how to monitor and deter them. *Network Security*, 8: 16–19, 2011.
2. Chen, Kuan-Ta, Jau-Yuan Chen, Chun-Rong Huang, and Chu-Song Chen, Fighting Phishing with Discriminative Keypoint Features of Webpages.
3. Sankhwar, Shweta, Dhirendra Pandey, and R. A. Khan, A glance of anti-phish techniques. *International Pure Applied and Mathematics*, 119(15): 2925–2936, 2018.

4. Sankhwar, Shweta and Dhirendra Pandey, Defending against phishing: Case studies. *International Journal of Advanced Research in Computer Science*, 8(5), 18–26, 2017.
5. Chandrasekaran, Madhusudhanan, Ramkumar Chinchani, and Shambhu Upadhyaya, Phoney: Mimicking user response to detect phishing attacks. *Proceedings of the 2006 International Symposium on World of Wireless, Mobile and Multimedia Networks*, Buffalo, NY, IEEE Computer Society, 2006.
6. Shah, Ripan, A proactive approach to preventing phishing attacks using Pshark. *Sixth International Conference on Information Technology: New Generations, 2009, ITNG'09*, Las Vegas, NV, IEEE, 2009.
7. Kim, Yonghwan, Shih-Hsien Hsu, and Homero Gil de Zúñiga, Influence of social media use on discussion network heterogeneity and civic engagement: The moderating role of personality traits. *Journal of Communication*, 63(3): 498–516, 2013.
8. Bedingfield, James and John Gehl, Automatic substitute uniform resource locator (URL) generation. U.S. Patent Application No. 11/290,407.
9. Berners-Lee, Tim, Larry Masinter, and Mark McCahill, Uniform resource locators (URL). No. RFC 1738, 1994.
10. Xiang, Guang, Jason Hong, Carolyn Penstein Rosé, Lorrie Cranor: A feature-rich machine learning framework for detecting phishing web sites. *ACM Transactions on Information and System Security (TISSEC)*, 14(2): 21, 2011.
11. Adedoyin-Olowe, Mariam, Mohamed Medhat Gaber, and Frederic Stahl. A survey of data mining techniques for social media analysis. arXiv preprint arXiv:1312.4617, 2013.
12. Chandrasekaran, Madhusudhanan, Krishnan Narayanan, and Shambhu Upadhyaya, Phishing email detection based on structural properties. *NYS Cyber Security Conference. Albany, NY*, 2–8, 2006
13. Sankhwar, Shweta, Dhirendra Pandey and Raees Ahmad Khan Email phishing: An enhanced classification model to detect malicious URLs, Scalable Information System ISSN no. 2032–9407, 2018.
14. Sankhwar Shweta, Dhirendra Pandey, and Raees Ahmad Khan, A step towards internet anonymity minimization: Cyber-crime investigation process perspective, In: Satapathy S. (Ed.) *Frontiers in Intelligent Computing: Theory and Application (FICTA), 2017*, Vol. 701. Springer Nature, London, 2018.
15. Hong, Jason. The state of phishing attacks. *Communications of the ACM* 55(1), 74–81, 2012.

CHAPTER 9

Big Data Digital Forensic and Cybersecurity

Pallavi Mishra

ICFAI Foundation for Higher Education

CONTENTS

9.1 INTRODUCTION

With the proliferation of the automation and telecommunication in almost all frontiers of human activity and with the ever-increasing number of IT users, the frequency of assaults (cyberattacks) to information systems (targets) is increasing by way of hacking, phishing, man-in-the-middle attacks, etc., resulting in damage and loss in large scale in terms of properties, reputation, human life and even the whole nation. As the extent of threat and damage increases, the need to resolve the solution also increases.

Due to digital growth and the consequential increase in computer frauds and cybercrimes, it poses a major challenge to law enforcement agencies on how to investigate these complex and sophisticated crimes. Digital forensics, a fairly new science of study, has provided the investigators with multipurpose tools to solve complex criminal cases [1]. The extreme addiction of people on the Internet increased the rate of cybercrimes to a larger extent due to which the job of digital forensic investigation has become more puzzling of the complexities involved in mining the potential evidences from the pool of big data.

The Internet offers an array of services to almost all the domains, and at the same time, it offers many open-source tools that are misused by criminals to commit computer frauds and cybercrime [2]. Based on the availability of tools, strategies and targets, different crimes in cyberspace have been classified. As the nature of cybercrimes and frauds varies, the technology adopted by forensic investigation also varies in order to timely respond to the cybercrimes by finding and analyzing the pieces of evidence in real time. Forensic investigation agencies need to gain expertise over the technology in order to anticipate the future crime.

Information warfare, as the name suggests, is information-centric warfare, which deals with the undesirable modification of the content of the information to victimize the opponent. It involves many proposed actions, military tactics, countermeasure techniques and weapons, which cause severe damage to information-dependent society, especially military operations.

One of the subsets of the information warfare, popularly known as cyber warfare, exists in various forms and deals with politically motivated attacks using advanced technologies to disrupt the fundamental interests of the political community such as state and nation. To combat the politically motivated attacks, digital forensics investigation adopts precise analytical and statistical techniques along with various investigation models for effective security measures.

Cyber defense system is developed to protect, prevent and defend the cyberattacks by providing timely responses to attack in order to safeguard assets. With the increasing number and sophistication of cybernetic attacks, the capacity to identify new threats and predict the nature of probabilistic unknown threats offers a vital means of self-defense. The forensic analyst examines and analyzes the computer security-related digital evidence and derives useful information to mitigate the system or network vulnerability.

The huge heterogeneous data sets (big data) are processed in roblem-solving time with the help of big data analytics tools, especially implemented in cybersecurity domain to discover relevant information (such as hidden patterns, unknown correlations) to identify any susceptibility to the targeted systems, which act as an aid for forensic investigation department to extract pieces of core evidence for further analysis and examination [3].

Big data analytics provides the cybersecurity professionals with modernized statistical tools and techniques to extract the data from multiple sources, to visualize and correlate the data for investigation purposes and draw the conclusion for further analysis. As a result, it increases efficiency in the analysis process that facilitates the detection of the early possibility of cyberattacks so that explicit actions can be executed to avoid and nullify the effects of the opponent's actions.

In reality, however, the complexity of the technology and the global nature of cyberspace make the detection of cybercrime difficult. In order to timely respond to cybercrimes, it requires proficiency to gather pieces of evidence, followed by appropriate procedures to examine and analyze and prove the crime which will be reported to the court of law for punishing cybercriminals.

This chapter is focused on the following major topics:

- Computer frauds and cybercrime,

- Taxonomy,

- Information warfare,

- Cyber warfare,

- Cyber defense systems,

- Big data analytics for cybersecurity.

9.2 COMPUTER FRAUDS AND CYBERCRIME

With the advancement of IT technology and digital growth, there have been revolutionary changes in all spheres of activities, and at the same time, it has widened a greater surface for cybercrimes and frauds in cyberspace.

Computer fraud is defined as network-based conflicts that involve illegal acts and practices in order to access the control over protected computer to gain valuable output by means of deception for one's own interest without any authorization.

Computer fraud is associated with various types of frauds under different schemes through chat rooms, email, etc. It also includes fraudulent transactions through websites made by different users, including financial institutions.

Cybercrime is an intentionally motivated offense committed in the cyberspace where most of the systems are connected globally. Thus, cybercrime mainly targets the computers, network-based devices and weak penetration points to perform malicious activities either to acquire benefits in terms of money or to exploit someone's reputation and fame [4].

The following are the factors that influence the growth of criminals on the Internet and the rate of cybercrime.

- The level of complexity and risk of cyberattacks are exponentially increasing that pose severe threats due to prevalent digital growth in cyberspace.

- The Internet facilities offer a wide array of services to all the domains. At the same time, it offers many tools free of cost and those that are misused by criminals to commit cybercrime.

- Technology-driven world has made possible commencement of cybercrime from any corner of the world without any necessity of physical presence.

- Availability of masking tools has become a boon for the cybercriminals to hide their identification and prevent themselves from being detected.

- Many users of electronic communication devices (ECD) are either unprotected or unaware of the threats that these devices are susceptible to while remaining connected to the Internet. This makes possible for cybercriminals to execute attacks with ease.

- Social media is a vital factor influencing cybercrimes, without proper verification of the content of the message; propaganda and disinformation are being spread to the target audience through social media (Facebook, WhatsApp, etc) either knowingly or unknowingly.

A fundamental principle of criminal law is that a crime consists of both mental (mens rea) and physical elements (actus reus).

With respect to cybercrime, the human actions (dynamic and varied in nature) in cyberspace, which laws seek to prevent, are the actus reus of cybercrime. Examples of such human actions include unauthorized access to other computing devices, hacking and sending viruses as attachments. Mens rea, on the other hand, refers to the "mental element of an offense" and constitutes an important element for a crime commission and imposition of penalty. Figure 9.1 shows the elements of the crime. For example, while hacking into devices, hackers do it with the intention of gaining unauthorized access, thereby committing cybercrime.

9.2.1 Tools Used in Cybercrime

Cybercriminals use various sophisticated tools and techniques for executing crimes by way of yielding the benefits of technology in several different ways. The following are the common tools used for committing computer frauds and cybercrime:

- **Proxy servers and anonymizer:** An anonymizer is a proxy server that makes Internet activity untraceable. It acts as an intermediate between the client and the server, which has a capability to bypass the firewall and access the information from the restricted server on the behalf of the actual user.

- **Password cracking:** It is a type of malware activity that attempts to gain illegal access control over the protected devices by compromising

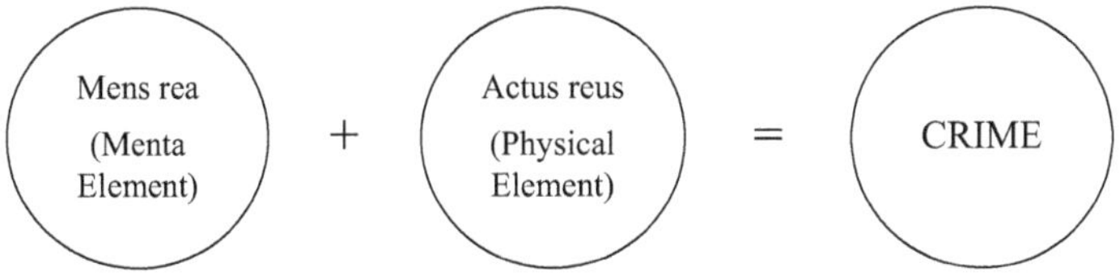

Mens rea (Menta Element) + Actus reus (Physical Element) = CRIME

FIGURE 9.1   Elements of crime.

security features and by adopting various sophisticated cracking tools and techniques.

- **Spywares:** Spywares is an infiltration software that is injected secretly to the targeted devices (victims), which aims to monitor unsuspecting users and their online activities. It intends to collect the personal and sensitive information about the targeted victim and tends to expose such sensitive data to an unauthorized person without any awareness of the victim.

- **Steganography:** It is an encryption technique of hiding secret data as such no one except the sender and the intended receiver could be aware of the encrypted data.

- **Trojan horse:** It is a malicious program that misleads users of its true content. It is designed to act as a spy on the victim and gain illegal access to the system to extract sensitive data.

- **Rogue security software:** It is a configuration of malware programs, which pretends to be an anti-malware software.

- **SQL injection:** It is a code injection technique that injects malicious codes on suspecting the vulnerabilities in the database layer of application.

- **Phishing:** Cybercriminals deceive people by making fake websites and using spoof emails to make them believe as if it is the original website. And finally after clicking on those fake links, the attackers can easily extract sensitive and personal information about the victim.

- **DoS attacks:** As its name suggests, it aims to deny the flow of services to cause either unavailability or reduction of availability of required services to the legitimate users by jamming the signals deliberately.

- **Social engineering:** It is a psychological manipulation of people's sensitiveness to giving out confidential information.

- **Man-in-the-middle attack:** The intruder secretly injects or alters the communication between the two end services by gaining private access and at the same time forming an illusion to the two parties that they are directly communicating without any third-party interception.

9.2.2 Cybercrime Statistics for 2018–2019

Statistical information pertaining to cyberattacks happened in recent years has been obtained from authentic reports (Figure 9.2) and highlighted as follows:

- Physical theft has been overpowered by information theft from 2017 onward. Information theft has become a violent threat to organizations in the present scenario. (ENISA Threat Landscape Report 2018)

- In 2018, there were millions of malware attacks, and about the maximum percentage of such attacks were miscellaneous that constantly change their identifiable features in order to evade detection, which makes it difficult for signature-based antivirus software programs to recognize, resulting in heavy iterations. From the current year up to April 2019, 24.55 million threats have so far been traced out. (2019 Web root Threat Report)

- More than 50% of the crimes committed in the United Kingdom are cybercrimes. (National Crime Agency)

- In every 39 s, the computers and the Internet are attacked by the malicious hackers. (University of Maryland)

- In 2018, a survey was conducted on different organizations and the report forecast that 78% of the organizations were affected by cyberattacks. (2019 Cyber threat Defense Report) (Figure 9.3)

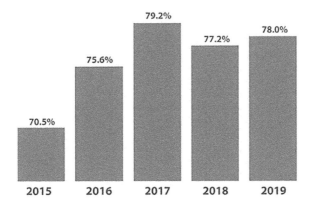

FIGURE 9.2   Frequency of successful attacks by year.

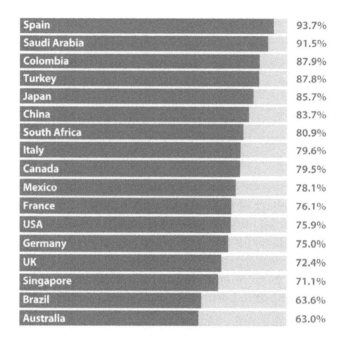

Spain	93.7%
Saudi Arabia	91.5%
Colombia	87.9%
Turkey	87.8%
Japan	85.7%
China	83.7%
South Africa	80.9%
Italy	79.6%
Canada	79.5%
Mexico	78.1%
France	76.1%
USA	75.9%
Germany	75.0%
UK	72.4%
Singapore	71.1%
Brazil	63.6%
Australia	63.0%

FIGURE 9.3   Percentage compromised by at least one successful attack in the past 12 months. (Source: Imperva 2019 Cyber threat Defense Report.)

9.3 TAXONOMY

The taxonomy of cybercrimes simplifies the complexity of varying terminologies related to similar crime patterns and organizes them according to their similarities [5,6], which is shown in Figure 9.4.

Various types of cybercrimes are as follows:

1. **Cyber violence:** The violence in the cyberspace tends to put the physical and mental well-being of the individual or group of individuals under threat. All the peripheral devices and the data that are linked to the Internet are mostly prone to cyber violence. There are umpteen number of cyber violence; among them, the most prevailing are as follows:

   • **Cyber world war:** As the name suggests, the battlefield in the virtual computer world which mainly targets the military and government sector intends to weaken the rival country's existing assets based on the Internet system, which are vital to a country's economic development and prosperity.

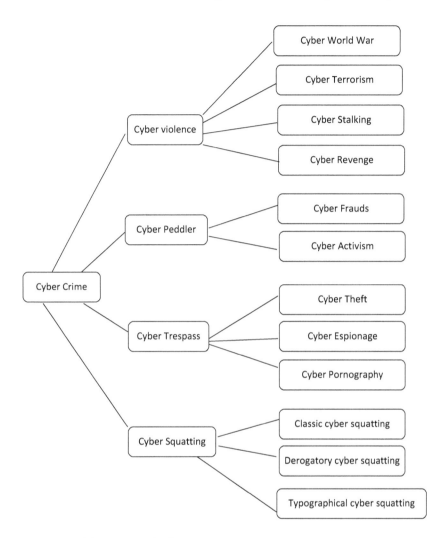

FIGURE 9.4   Taxonomy of cybercrime.

- **Cyberterrorism:** It is a deliberately planned attack, which takes place with the use of the Internet to disrupt the victim in terms of financial loss, threaten or result in loss of life in order to achieve the political and ideological game.

- **Cyberstalking:** It is a serious crime where the attacker makes frequent use of electronic and communication devices to harass a victim by false accusation, identification theft, trapping of physical locations and data manipulation and distortion by sending a virus to the target system.

- **Cyber revenge:** This type of attack is purely intended to harm the reputation of the enemies by means of unethical behaviors such as disclosing the confidential information and disrupting the computer-based resources and infrastructures.

2. **Cyber peddler:** It is a criminal practice that aims to steal the confidential and sensitive information of an individual or a group with the help of Internet technology. It is categorized into two types:

- **Cyber fraud:** It is a criminal offense that heavily relies on the interconnected communication technology to attack globally connected devices in order to deceit the information through social engineering techniques to the targeted victims for the sole purpose of monetary games.

- **Cyber activism:** In this type of crime, the misuse of the Internet and communication-based technologies exists, such as Twitter, Facebook, YouTube, LinkedIn, WhatsApp and Gmail, for spreading rumors to damage their rival reputation by misleading information about them to achieve personal benefits.

3. **Cyber trespass:** It is unlawful access to the computer system with an intent to gain financial information and other services that infringe confidentiality and moral primitives of cybersecurity. The various types of cyber trespass are as follows:

- **Cyber theft:** It aims to plunder valuable and confidential records of the victim for illegal purposes.
  Cyber theft is categorized into two types.

  a. **Theft to cyberspace:** Cyberspace is one of the most critical domains, which may prone to cyberattack unless maintaining an aerial perspective (bird's eye view) on the ongoing activities on cyberspace. Cyberattackers aim to make congestion to the cyberspace in order to disrupt the network services or to gain unauthorized access.

  b. **Theft to data/information:** Data theft is a growing phenomenon that involves the stealing of confidential records and sensitive data. Cybersecurity is one of the most concerned aspects of any nation's prosperity and economic development.

The fundamental of cybersecurity involves the confidentiality, integrity and availability of information in real time, which should be protected from the intruders.

- **Cyber espionage:** It aims to procure confidential records illegally by tracking the activity of individual, company and organization, by performing malicious activities on the network.

- **Cyber pornography:** It is an unethical act that makes use of cyberspace for exposing obscene materials to the targeted victims. As a result of these illegal actions, it may lead to the loss of self-esteem of the victim, and even his/her life may get into danger.

4. **Cyber squatting:** It is an act of illegal registration of domain name containing the trademark that has a narrow resemblance to the original domain, which causes an illusion among the users. Its main objective is to gain monetary advantage from the goodwill of the trademark.

   - **Classic cyber squatting:** The objective of the cyber squatter is to get ransom from his targeted victim in order to release the illegally registered domain that has been occupied by the squatter.

   - **Derogatory cyber squatting:** The cyber squatter intends to hamper the status of the targeted domain name through illegal actions such as uploading the obscene images, hate speech and violated content on the targeted domain.

   - **Typographical cyber squatting:** The cyber squatter deliberately registers the preexisting domain with a slight manipulation with a similar trademark for monetary gain.

9.4 INFORMATION WARFARE

Information warfare is associated with the conflicting activities undertaken by a predator to manipulate the information without the knowledge of the victim, and the predators gain advantages unfairly by exerting control over the victim. Prediction and identification of such a conspiracy are not feasible to be assessed in real time leading to massive exploitation.

The manipulation, degradation and denial of information are done strategically by the perpetrator using various malicious techniques to gain an unfair advantage over the victims. The perpetrator exploits the adversary information and information systems while defending and preserving the integrity of his own information systems from exploitation.

The activity of information warfare includes the following:

- Gathering of strategic facts and figures,

- Examining the correctness of the collected data,

- Propagating false and exaggerated information and ideas to discourage and degrade the opponent's power and actions,

- Undercutting the importance and gravity of the information of the victim,

- Restricting the enemy from accessing the relevant data.

9.4.1 The Basic Strategies in Information Warfare

The information warfare can be used for both defensive and offensive purposes. Offensive information warfare seeks dominance over the enemy's information, computer information systems and control systems using a myriad of tools. Defensive information warfare seeks to preserve the nation's ability to protect its national information infrastructure, which depends on the ability to detect, correct and recover from attacks.

The basic strategies of information warfare include the following:

I. **Denial of information:** The main objective is to restrict the opponent from accessing useful information from the channel either by introducing noise into the communicating channel using various advanced techniques, such as jamming and overloading, or by manipulating and distorting the original information that closely resembles the background noise of the information.

II. **Deception and mimicry:** The primary goal is to intentionally provide propaganda and disinformation to an opponent with a motive to deceive him. The device attempts to mimic a signal, familiar to the victim, giving the false belief to the opponent so as the victim will take decisions against his own interest that indirectly favors the attacker.

III. **Disruption and destruction:** It intends to disrupt the opponent's information receiver devices in order to prevent them from receiving any information. Disruption behavior intends to disrupt the information receiver services temporarily, whereas destruction behavior attempts to exploit its services permanently.

IV. **Subversion:** It is the most complex strategy of information warfare, which involves the insertion of malicious codes into the opponent's system, which creates a backdoor that would trigger a self-destructive process such as logic bomb, a virus that tends to corrupt and disable the functionalities of the system.

9.4.2 Various Forms of Information Warfare

Information warfare can be of seven different forms, which are as follows:

1. **Command and control:** It is an application of information operation, especially in defense forces. The command and control warfare disrupts the interlinking flow of commands (command structure) from their associated wings by putting a barrier between their linkages.

2. **Intelligence-based warfare:** Intelligence-based warfare system is inbuilt with photoconductive cells (sensors) that possess the capability to gather and analyze data and communicate with other systems. By this technique, it corrupts the configurations and functionalities of the target system. At the same time, it facilitates protecting its own information system, thus preventing them from attack.

3. **Electronic warfare:** It is a warfare equipped with radio frequency spectrum that disables the enemy's electronics devices by creating confusion signals in the path of the enemy using laser lights and radio signals. It can also sense and detect missile attacks by intercepting attacking signals.

4. **Psychological warfare:** It is a warfare intended to reduce an opponent's morale to achieve its own interests by influencing the emotions, motives and behavior of the victims; at the same time, it protects its own set of combat direction systems.

5. **Hacker warfare:** Hacker warfare is an attack on the computer system using different hacking tricks and strategies. The approaches and techniques adopted during this warfare vary depending upon the perception and mindset of the hacker in terms of gaining fun

and pleasure upon succeeding in hacking, or to fulfilling the intention to paralyze or crash someone's system.

6. **Economic information warfare:** With the help of this warfare, a potential threat can be created against a nation by using economic means, which aims to weaken the targeted nation's economic and financial background, thereby reducing the strength of the evolving relation between political and military power.

7. **Cyber warfare:** The technology-driven world has become vulnerable for the entire nation, which is implicitly providing a platform with new opportunities for the commencement of cyber warfare. This is a warfare generated by the aggressive use of advanced technologies with a view to damage the communication system of the enemy, resulting in which the victim sustains heavy loss in its fundamental interests.

9.5 CYBER WARFARE

Cyber warfare is intended to attack the computer and information system of the rival country with an ill political motive. This is a warfare deliberately framed by violent use of modernized tools and methodologics to attack the targeted country, especially for strategic or military purposes [7–9]. Thus, it poses a very real and significant threat to a nation's national security and interests.

The most fundamental interests of political communities are as follows:

- To establish peace, tranquility and security;
- To avail requisite assets;
- To remain independent;
- To bring and intensify qualitative economic reforms.

9.5.1 Forms of Cyber Warfare

Cyber warfare, which gives insight knowledge of the extent of the severity of the consequences upon implementation, can take one of the three forms:

i. Espionage (the act of finding out secret information about other countries using the Internet),

ii. The spread of disinformation (false information spread deliberately to deceive others),

iii. Sabotage (destruction of targeted devices, which are responsible to satisfy the fundamental interest of a nation).

With the proliferation of cyberattacks along with their increased complexity involved in the methodologies adopted by the attackers, cyber defense is inevitable to protect the information and other assets from undesirable disclosure. With an objective to acquire knowledge about a specific domain, cyber defense plays a significant role in analysis, mitigates the possible future attacks or threats on a given environment and thus frames the strategy necessary to counteract the cyberattacks.

9.6 CYBER DEFENSE SYSTEMS

The term "cyber defense" has been derived from the words "cyber" and "defense", which are its elemental words. The word cyber, abbreviated for cyberspace, forms a virtual world by an interconnection of links between the computers, Internet-enabled devices and the other network-based infrastructure along with information assets. The defense is the proactive act that is deliberately practiced to combat and overcome the issue of computer-related crimes in order of merit to safeguard assets of a nation from attack.

Cyber defense is a mechanism that enhances the capabilities of using security strategies and resources in an effective manner. It ensures flawless operations without any interruption arising out of threat. In the modern approach, cyber defense system emerges with a new concept of active cyber defense that mitigates the cyber threats and vulnerabilities by discovering the threats, studying their capabilities and analyzing for mitigation [7].

Cyber defense has accomplished the following systematic and logical analysis to figure out the possibility of future attacks and the target points in order to execute early defense mechanisms to protect from cyberattacks.

1. **Cyber sensors and exploitation:** It is a technology applied to evaluate and determine action plans drawn by the attackers and their ability to exploit during the active process involving critical functions.

2. **Cyber situation awareness:** Situational awareness in the cyber domain provides a broad and explicit perspective of threats and susceptibility by predicting the mission outcome.

3. **Cyber defensive mechanism:** It is equipped with various tools with hidden codes, scanners and software to counter the threats relating to secret messages, viruses and unauthorized access.

4. **Cyber command and control:** It is a technology-driven mechanism that systematically plans and coordinates the information derived from the situational awareness element to build up defensive practices. This mechanism analyzes the situation, explores the possible options and evaluates the required decision at once. Simultaneously, it communicates and implements the planned actions.

5. **Cyber strategies and tactics:** It is an important knowledge guiding tool that determines the accuracy of proactive decisions taken on a particular attack situation on the basis of which the action plans are designed in a systematic and sequential agreed manner. It also acts as a guiding tool for necessary changes in the decision as per necessity.

6. **Cyber science and engineering:** It is the cornerstone that facilitates getting insight into knowledge of the framework, anatomy, building and maintenance of the strong combat system.

In order to achieve a viable cyber defense capability, the following above advancements are required in the field of science and technology for effective implementation in cyber defense mechanism.

9.7 BIG DATA ANALYTICS FOR CYBERSECURITY

Traditional security analytics (first-generation Security Information and Event Management, SIEM) is a reactive security approach, in which actions were taken after the visualization of a sign of threats. The traditional approach of analytics for cybersecurity was confined to only derive a relationship between data at a network-level application. These conservative approaches where rules were defined manually by security experts were impotent and inefficient to understand the human activity and thus liable to adapt to their dynamic behavioral changes.

Traditional rule-based systems are thus incompetent to handle the complexity of advanced attacks and the dynamic nature of user behavior. As such, security experts, who supervise the maintenance and regulation of security, think like a hacker and anticipate all master plans of the hackers. They take countermeasures in order to protect their vital assets and information. However, reactive security would be effective in case the time complexity of the perpetrator to perform damage would exceed the time complexity of the defense system to take defense actions. Since attackers use automated and targeted methods, reactive security method is no longer effective.

Big data analytics (second-generation SIEM) is a proactive security approach, which is designed to handle big data, which correlates events based on combined data from logs and other sources, in near real-time, detecting indicators of suspicious activity. It uses advanced data analytics techniques and predictive models to gather, categorize and analyze information and data gathered from multiple network devices to detect advanced threats in real time. Big data analytics tools are sophisticated and especially implemented for forensic investigation, which provides information about the origin of an attack, how it happened and the extent of the damage [10]. Unlike traditional security tools, it helps to identify suspicious activities, detect insider threats and monitor user behavior in real time.

Big data tools are widely implemented in various organizations, enterprises, etc to identify and explore new possibilities and opportunities, resulting in strategic decision-making. As such, it has brought a significant evolutionary change in the field of security – intelligence domain by minimizing the time for integrating and investigating various relevant pieces of evidence related to cybercrime as well as mapping the patterns of historical records for forensic purposes.

Big data analytics in cybersecurity has the expertise to gather a huge amount of digital data in order to draw accurate insights using statistical techniques, predictive models and artificial intelligence (AI) that can improve the effectiveness to predict the cyber threats at an initial phase.

In other words, big data analytics with the help of advanced analytic and statistical techniques treats way to examine different sources of data, extract in-depth knowledge through heterogeneous data and provide insightful information through unknown correlations and data sources in real time, which helps digital forensic investigators in making faster analysis of data and informed decisions [11,12].

The rapid evolution in the technology of big data analytics provides a new standard and finds ways to solve the big data storage issue, processing and analysis by using sophisticated tools and techniques.

9.7.1 Modern Techniques of Big Data Analytics

Data fusion and data integration: It is the method of integrating significant data from disparate sources with an objective to draw insights from the historical records, data sources, etc in order to recognize the patterns of suspicious behavior, to detect anomalies in cyberspace.

Machine learning: The subset of AI includes statistical techniques. It can be used for the data analysis process that deals with computer algorithms to produce assumptions in the field of cybersecurity and forensic investigation. It provides predictions on the basis of their assumptions that would be impossible for human analysts.

Data mining: It is an interdisciplinary field (including statistics and many other scientific fields) with an objective to discover relevant and meaningful patterns from the diversified data sets in order to generate new and exciting knowledge and information. It plays a vital role in the extraction of hidden patterns, relevant information regarding the cyber threats from historical records and sources of raw data, and thus provides insights in order to detect and prevent cyberattacks [11].

9.7.2 Tools Used in Big Data Analytics

The analysts take the help of many advanced tools to generate complex queries and apply machine learning algorithms on top of Hadoop, which enables parallel distributed processing of voluminous data (big data). Other big data tools are Pig, which is a scripting language especially useful for solving complex queries, Hive, Mahout and RHadoop.

Analytics can guide network controllers and regulators especially for the supervision of real-time network streaming and detection of cautious patterns, which provides risk and security management intelligence to the fraud detection mechanism.

The applications of big data analytics help data scientists, predictive modelers, statisticians and other potential analysts to examine the yielding volume of structured (name, age, gender, dates, etc.), semi-structured (.csv files, html code) and unstructured data (audio, video files, emails, etc), which facilitates taking effective and appropriate decisions in real time, which were earlier a strenuous and prolonged task with minimum accuracy using traditional analytical approach.

9.7.3 Big Data Analytics: A Modern Approach

The technological advances in storage, processing and analysis of big data have brought big differences between traditional analytics and big data analytics, which are as follows:

a. The traditional data warehouses are liable to store data for the long term, while big data applications are capable to retain data indefinitely to analyze the historical correlations to detect cyber threats.

b. Big data tools, such as Hadoop ecosystem and NoSQL database, handle big data and increase the efficiency to solve complex queries and analysis. These tools enhance the adaptability and cost-effectiveness of dedicated space centers.

c. The advancement in the technology, especially for storage and processing of big data, has become possible because of Hadoop, which facilitates vast storage with parallel computing. The transformation of data using ETL (extract, transform and load) process in the case of traditional warehouse is rigid which users require to define schemas; thus, incorporating new schema is difficult.

The advanced technologies adopted by big data analytics have transformed the performance in security analytics by

a. Gathering of voluminous heterogeneous data from various sources,

b. Performing a systematic and deep analysis of the data to predict suspicious activity,

c. Providing a visual representation of information based on security analysis and examination,

d. Attaining real-time analysis of data, which makes possible for users to draw conclusion deliberately and facilitates a faster decision-making process.

The third generation of SIEM, proposed by Gartner in 2017, incorporated the traditional SIEM potential along with two new technologies providing the following upgraded features of big data analytics.

- User and entity behavior analytics (UEBA) is a mechanism that records the workflow of the users with the help of machine learning techniques and detects any anomalies deviating from normal patterns. Modern SIEMs surpass correlations by taking advantage of machine learning and AI methods to identify and explore typical and atypical human behaviors. This insight can help organizations discover malicious activity, insider threats and fraud.

- Security automation, orchestration and response (SOAR) is an act of integrating disparate technologies and connecting security tools in order to make them capable of working together, which facilitates security analysts to instantly investigate incidents and automatically respond to an incident. Next-generation SIEMs now include automated incident response systems. For example, the SIEM could identify and alert for ransomware and respond by automatically implementing containment steps on affected systems, before the hacker encrypts the data.

BIBLIOGRAPHY

1. Raghavan, Sriram. Digital forensic research: Current state of the art. *CSI Transactions on ICT* (2013) 1.1, 91–114.
2. Ahmad, Atif, Sean B. Maynard, and Sangseo Park. Information security strategies: Towards an organizational multi-strategy perspective. *Journal of Intelligent Manufacturing* (2014) 25(2) 357–370.
3. Das, Dolly, Urjashee Shaw, and Smriti Priya Medhi. Realizing digital forensics as a big data challenge. *4th International Conference on "Computing for Sustainable Global Development*, New Delhi, India, 01–03 March (2017).
4. Bregant, Jessica, and Robert Bregant. Cybercrime and computer crime. *The Encyclopedia of Criminology and Criminal Justice* (2014) 5, 1–5.
5. Brar, Harmandeep Singh, and Gulshan Kumar. Cybercrimes: A proposed taxonomy and challenges. *Journal of Computer Networks and Communications* (2018) 2018, 11.
6. Poonia, A. Singh. Cyber crime: Challenges and its classification. *International Journal of Emerging Trends and Technology in Computer Science (IJETTCS)* (2014) 2, 2278–6856.
7. Galinec, Darko, Darko Možnik, and Boris Guberina. Cybersecurity and cyber defence: National level strategic approach. *Automatika: časopis za automatiku, mjerenje, elektroniku, računarstvo i komunikacije* (2017) 58.3, 273–286.
8. Wang, Lidong, and Cheryl Ann Alexander. Big data in distributed analytics, cybersecurity, cyber warfare and digital forensics. *Digital Technologies* (2015) 1.1, 22–27.
9. Dejey S., and S. Murugan. *Cyber Forensics Book*. Oxford University Press, New Delhi (2018).
10. Zawoad, Shams, and Ragib Hasan. Digital forensics in the age of big data: Challenges, approaches, and opportunities. *2015 IEEE 17th International Conference on High Performance Computing and Communications, 2015 IEEE 7th International Symposium on Cyberspace Safety and Security, and 2015 IEEE 12th International Conference on Embedded Software and Systems*. IEEE, 2015. New York, NY, USA.

11. Kantarcioglu, Murat, and Bowei Xi. Adversarial data mining: Big data meets cyber security. *Proceedings of the 2016 ACM SIGSAC Conference on Computer and Communications Security*, Vienna, Austria, ACM (2016).
12. Mohammed, Hussam, Nathan Clarke, and Fudong Li. An automated approach for digital forensic analysis of heterogeneous big data. *Journal of Digital Forensics* (2016) 11, 137–152.

Index

Embedded sensors, 49
EnCase toolkit, 32–33, 59
Encrypted Big Query Client, 97
Encrypted database, 96–97
Ensemble learning, 144
Enterprise environs, 175–176
Entity integrity, 99
Exogenous transition, 113–114
Extract, transform, load (ETL) tools,
 147, 201

F

Feature subset selection, 140
Finite State Machine (FSM), 112, 115, 116
Flume, 76, 77
Forensic investigation process, 13–14
 phases of, 14–15
  analysis, 17
  collection, 16–17
  identification, 15–16
  presentation, 17–18
  readiness, 14–15
Forensic logbook, 166–167
Forensic science, 23, 56
Forensic toolkit (FTK), 33–34, 59, 153
FSM, *see* Finite State Machine (FSM)
FTK, *see* Forensic toolkit (FTK)
Fusion-based digital investigation model,
 162–164, 169
 data collection and preprocessing, 165
 data estimation phase, 166
 decision-level fusion, 166
 as evidence acquiring medium,
  167, 168
 forensic logbook, 166–167
 high-level fusion, 166
 look-up table, 165
 low-level fusion, 165
 mapping Phases of, 168
 objective of, 167–168
 sources of, 164
 user interface, 167

G

Gartner analytic ascendancy model, 135
Guidance Software, 4, 32

H

Hacker warfare, 195–196
Hadoop, 200
 architecture layers, 67–68
 chain of custody, 83–84
 components of, 68–70
 data analysis tools
  Flume, 76, 77
  HBase, 73–74
  Hive, 72–73
  Pig, 74–75
  Sqoop, 75–76
 distributed process, 68–69
 evidence sources of, 76–79
  data collection, 79–81, 83
  structured and unstructured
   data, 81–83
 host-working framework, 67
 internals of, 65–67
Hadoop distributed file system (HDFS),
 68, 70–73, 148
HBase, 73–74, 78–79
HDFS, *see* Hadoop distributed file
  system (HDFS)
Health care
 big data for, 45–47
  advantages of, 55–56
  challenges, 50–51
  digital forensics, 56–60
  digitization, 51–55
  evaluation and interpretation, 48
  forensic science and, 56
  output and accessibility,
   54–55
  pattern developments, 47
  result and usage, 48
  technological application,
   60–61
  value-added tool, 48–50
 business analysis of, 46
 decision making, 49
 system segmentation, 49
Hibernation file, 11
High-level fusion, 166
Hive, 72–73
Homomorphic encryption, 96

For Product Safety Concerns and Information please contact our EU
representative GPSR@taylorandfrancis.com
Taylor & Francis Verlag GmbH, Kaufingerstraße 24, 80331 München, Germany

www.ingramcontent.com/pod-product-compliance
Ingram Content Group UK Ltd.
Pitfield, Milton Keynes, MK11 3LW, UK
UKHW021119180425
457613UK00005B/156